Sandy nice to

Sgt. P Macdonald

Marine Corps Gallantry

or

Psychosis

author

A.S. Macdonald

A special thanks to the editor
Cathy Short

A.S.M. Publications
465 Packers falls Rd.
Lee NH 03824

ISBN 0-9676941-0-8

For information address ASM publisher

465 Packersfalls rd Lee NH 03824

Printed United States of America
On the web at

www.abnormalart.com

Table of contents

Dedication

I would like to
dedicate this book to my
wife, Agnes and
my three daughters
Susan,
Tracy, Lynne, for
the joy and tolerance
they
have given me
over the years Thank You

Introduction

I would like to start this book with a present-day acknowledgement of what you are about to read. I was discharged honorably from the Marine Corps over twenty years ago. My adjustment back to a non-military life took over fifteen years. Because of a car accident, I completely lost my memory of everything prior to my eighteenth birthday. I grew from an infant to a Marine Sergeant in the four years it took to complete my Marine tour.

At the end of this book, I arrive back in my hometown of Alton, New Hampshire. In my years away from Alton, I read many things in letters about local events. My mother as well as several girls corresponded with me on a regular basis. I believe that at least once I came home on leave from the Marines to the town of Alton for thirty days. But I have no memory. The people who wrote me letters were special to me. I lived for these letters. They gave me the belief that I had a life other than the Marine Corps.

My mind expanded during my four years in the Marine Corps. I had to adjust. I had to accept the fact I had a limited brain function. I was unaware that I was different from other people. I learned within the structured environment of the Marines how to live and survive.

My adjustment back into civilian life was not easy. We live in a non-structured society. People do and say what they feel is correct. The laws that govern the civilian population can be interpreted in a wide range. I started my life as a civilian trying understand reality. I attended college part time for eight years. While in college, volunteering became important to me. I needed a way to feel I was giving something back for having been allowed to come home alive. I started volunteering with the American Cancer Society. While doing this one-day a week, I began volunteering at two hospitals. After eleven years I switched to volunteering at schools, state, county and local government departments.

One of the schools I volunteered at is in Wakefield, New Hampshire. I teach what is called a "trashformation class." I demonstrate to schoolchildren how to use what is discarded as trash to fix or make things. And I tell the children about a couple of events in my Marine career. One was the fact that I used the toilet seat to fix a two hundred and seventy-two million-dollar piece of equipment. This amazes the children. Then I explain how I fixed an Okinawan farmer's manure spreader with the "S" hook from a bungie cord. This helps the kids to understand that anything can be fixed.

My only memory of my Marine career was these two stories. For a long time, I had no need to remember any other part of the events of those years. Then a boy (named Dustin) in one of my Wakefield classes said he thought my days in the Marine Corps were important. He suggested I write these stories down so my family and others in the state can read them. I did not think I was capable of doing this. It was a challenge. A mission to teach others what I grew to believe in. I took the challenge into my thoughts. I talked to many people about the idea. Everyone was supportive of the mission, although my daughter said, "Daddy you don't even read books-how you going to write one?" That inspired me to attempt a book from events in a lost memory.

I spent the next fourteen days writing this book. My wife describes how my personality changed as I got into recalling my memory. I researched my many photo albums of the Marine Corps days. I read letters and notes to recall events. I read pages of disciplinary charges placed against me over the time. Each event or memory would flash into my mind all at once. Suddenly, I could remember the smallest detail and see the faces of the people involved. Sometimes I felt happy, other times sad. A few times my eyes got moist with thoughts as they appeared. Other times I remembered the long lonely hours I spent wondering, "Why?" Just as fast as the memories appeared, they left me. I wrote each event down as quickly and accurately as I could.

This book is a true story of my life in the Marine Corps. The events occurred from November 1970 to November 1974; I was in the Corps for a four-year tour. I have no precise memory of the time span that each event happens. The times of my promotions or transfers did not stay with me. I wrote the book from my sequences of transfer from one country to the next. I know which country each event occurred, but not the exact day or how long a time span it took to be completed.

The amazing thing is I still have amnesia. My mental function is still limited. I do not remember from day to day. I start new every day. Even if I meet someone I know, I have to work to remember who this person is. Each time I start a job, I have no way of knowing if I know how to do the job. I will try most any job, because I do not know that I cannot. Each time I start one of my volunteer classes, I do not know what to say. I walk into the classroom with a box of junk and the pages of my mind open. I start talking describing past events about my experiences. The words just come to me on what I am talking about. Talking while using models and demonstrating my description I am able to talk about subjects from my past. A day or so later the pages of my mind will close until the next time the memory is retrieved.
Here is my story.

Chapter two: A small NH town

Alton, New Hampshire in the 1960's was a two and a half-hour drive north of Boston. People who worked hard in Boston went to Alton for vacation. This was how city folks enjoyed the easy life of no stress, just fun and relaxation. It was a quiet drive along long stretches of highways lined with thick forest. Occasionally a farmhouse appeared through the trees or a road off the highway. There would be seven kids with our parents in this one car escaping the city trying to enjoy the freedom. The drive to Alton was relaxing except for an occasional flare up between the kids riding in the back seat.

There are three main roads from Boston to Alton New Hampshire. Both interstate 95 to Portsmouth NH and route 16 are four-lane highways. They both lead north along the Maine border. The next leg of the trip is on route 11 going west. In 1960 this was a new state highway with wide hot-topped breakdown lanes on both sides. At the end of this road you are within fifteen miles of the town of Alton. The new highway ends at a barricade and a detour sign with arrows pointing left and right. On the left is a little shack like building with a sign: Dot's Lunch. To the right is route 11 with a sign for Alton, NH. This is a small country road disguised as a state highway. The road first becomes Main Street in the town of New Durham. Main Street consists of a church, a single car garage (called the fire station) and a farmhouse with a sign over the door that says Town Clerk. The speed of all cars drops to a crawl, as regulars fear being stopped by a country policeman. The slow speed does not add much to your time in this town. The town line is only a couple hundred feet away. Main Street in New Durham ends after the third building. Then route 11 turns into a single lane tarred road winding through the hills for five miles. When you reach the intersection of route 28, 11, and 16, you are at the edge of Main Street in Alton, New Hampshire.

In the 1960's Alton was a town of about two thousand residents. The core area of Alton was like a small city. The buildings were all bunched together on small lots. The first businesses you saw were a funeral parlor and the electric power office building, hidden between people's homes. Next to the funeral parlor, a large cemetery that added to the open space of the congested area. Single-family homes, within arms' reach of each other dominated the center of town. A gas station was situated on the left next to a grocery store. Across the street was the town hall, a large two-story brick building; the second floor is one large room for town meetings. The local 5&10 cents store was located beside the grass common area around a flagpole in front of the town hall. The Catholic Church, one of many churches in town, was across the street next to the only self-serve laundromat in town.

Main Street ends, but the road continues as route 11 to the bay area on Lake Winnipesaukee. The single-family houses line the street on both sides. The residents here are the year round people -- locals-- who make their income from the vacationers. The locals have named different sections of town. These are not official designated areas but names the residents use to describe where their house is located. Some of these areas are separated by three to six mile drives on a state highway.

South Alton is an isolated section of the town that is closer to another town to the north. Only the people, who lived there, traveled out that far because of its isolated location. "The mountain," short for Alton Mountain, is where most of the original families from Alton lived. The mountain was a place for the local kids to drink and swim in the river with out adults around. West Alton is about six miles a long the West Side of the bay to the lake. This area was cool but so far away that we only went for special reasons. East Alton was six miles along the other side of the bay. This area was comprised of large boring tracts of land. The people of Alton were nice people. All the people in the world are nice, if you can just overlook the unlikable parts. The off season would start the first week of September and this small New Hampshire town would close up shop and almost look like a ghost town.

My parent's farm was half way to the east section of town. You went three miles toward East Alton and Lily Pond Road was on your right. My parents had a forty-five acres to raise their seven children on. We named this place the Lucky Seven Farm. It was located half a mile up a narrow dirt road with only one other house. We were isolated except for a retired couple's summer house located near the beginning of Lily Pond Road. We lived in a large red farmhouse with five bedrooms and a long country porch. The barn was attached to the house by a breezeway. Off a distance in the back yard was a large chicken coop building. A movable pigpen was sometimes located out there. We had several large gardens taking up several acres of land.

My father was raised a strict Roman Catholic. He was tough on the boys. A loving father and mother ruled our family of one girl and six boys. We did everything together as a family. One of the effects of living in an isolated place is that parents can control friends. The times were not tough for our family. We had what was necessary to live a comfortable life. The luxury items were few, but we had no need for them. We raised meat, vegetables, and eggs to feed the family through each year. My father worked as a carpenter, master electrician, and master plumber, sometimes locally. He also sometimes worked at jobs far away, and was on the road days at a time.

We always had what we needed, but my father tried not to buy unnecessary things for us boys to do our chores with. Tools were available for all jobs, but if a tool got lost or broken there was a price to pay. We boys learned to repair everything with what ever was handy. My brothers and I would be required to complete our chores with not considering the amount of time it took. Repairing a tool or finding a more efficient way to finish the task meant more time for things we wanted to do. The difficulty of completing a chore was up to the person doing the job. My brothers and I worked late into the evening completing chores that we had not completed when we were told to do them. It was a matter of survival because food and sleep was deprived until the job was finished correctly.

My father brought an old junk car home one day for my twin brother and me. It wasn't much of a car. The bottom of one of the seats touched the ground. Some of the windows were broken; there were no headlights. My brother and I didn't care. Twin nine-year-old boys accept any car.

The deal with the car was that my brother and I had to make it into a farm truck. We could use our imagination in chopping the roof off or any thing else, but it had to work. The other choice was to do the work around the farm by hand. The first thing we did was stick a board under the seat to hold it off the ground. Boys and their imagination created quite the ugly working vehicle. A few weeks after the truck was finished, it lost its appeal. Work was pretty much all we could do with it. The number of jobs kept on increasing. We went out in the woods to get firewood, hauled rocks out of the gardens, or found ways to repair things. There was no end. We knew before my father would allow us into the house that all our jobs had to be completed each day.

Punishment was a different story. My father loved each and every one of us always. He was going to make sure we knew right from wrong. Obedient kids were good kids, so we were going to obey all rules. If we broke a rule the punishment had to deter future wrongs. This man worked long hard hours at his jobs. He would come home at night in time for dinner when he was not on the road. Dinner was on the table at the same time every night. Dad's question at dinner would always be, "Anything bad I need to know about?" The person who did something wrong would always squirm in his chair because that child knew if a confession did not come forth some one would tell. We knew what was going to happen after dinner that night to the one in trouble. Each of us had to finish everything on our plate each night. The bad child could find it hard to belong to the clean plate club, as it was called.

After dinner and the chore of dishes, whoever was in trouble went to their room. The long wait while doing our homework or just reading could be one or two hours of silent thinking. A scared look would come over our faces when the bedroom door opened. My father would come into the room and ask you, "What did you do that was wrong?" He would discuss it with us. Then he would say, "Stand up and pull your pants down." He took his leather belt off his waist and hit our bare butt as we laid over the edge of the bed. The blisters and bruised flesh hurt to no end. You knew when the beating was over because he always said the same thing, "This hurts me worse than it hurts you."

This was not child abuse. It was the discipline of the times. The process of punishment was not intended to be mean, but to teach right from wrong. My father, was and is a kind loving man who did things as he learned from his father. He made mistakes, but don't we all?

My mother held the family together. She would protect and did anything for her kids. Our house, even with seven kids, was always spotless. My mother cooked bread and desserts while we were in school. After school she helped us with our homework and reminded us to do our chores. I don't believe she had a driver's license because she was usually at home. Her encouraging words helped us when something broke: "Use what you can to get that fixed before your father gets home". My mother disapproved of the harsh punishment but accepted it because she believed it would make us a better person.

I was a happy sometimes-scared little boy until I reached the age of seventeen, raised in a little town, isolated by family life on a farm. At seventeen, I was about to be a senior in high school. I had a driver's license and a summer job at the fish fry down by the lake. I could now test the waters of life on my own. The town of Alton had grown and changed by the end of the sixties to be larger with more businesses and a more diverse population.

When I was a senior in high school, life seemed so confining. I was like most other children at this time in their lives. We have to bend the rules. My senior class was the largest in Alton history. There were twenty-nine other students and myself in the class. I was the smallest male in height and weight in the class. My small size made me want to be recognized by others. I joked, teased and took a lot of crazy chances to be noticed. Identified by adults as "having potential," they thought I could be saved. (Not that I was a bad person but as a kid I never lived up to what was expected of me). My grade point average in school was around D-C and never exceeded that. In my senior year, I sought excitement, and that led to trouble.

Love mixed with a teenage boy revolting against life cannot be good. The slow, boring off-season was in full bloom, as November was ending. This time of year meant deer hunting season was at hand. The men would hunt during the day and drink at night. The boys would go to school part of the day, then go hunting. The hunting always ended at dark for everybody so this is when chores were done. The women would take care of the house, and if a chance for affection passed by they were known to indulge themselves.

On November twentieth I attended school but planned on leaving early to hunt. Noontime, which meant lunch, was when three male friends and I left the school grounds at separate times. We all met at a friend's car that was parked just off school grounds. Once everyone was in the car we headed toward the bay. We four seventeen-year-old boys each popped open a beer as we drove toward Alton

Mountain. The best place to drink and get ready to go hunting was the Back Bay beach on the church grounds. The church grounds have a ten thousand-person community of run down shacks called cabins. In the summer the church grounds filled up with religious wives and children while husbands stayed home and work. This religious retreat was located at the base of Alton Mountain and acted as a border between the mountain and bay area. This hideaway gave us a private place to drink, to load our weapons and to leave the car while we hunted. Today we realize the problems of mixing drinking, driving, and hunting. This was the way in the area I lived, was acceptable to the young adults.

The four of us were surprised when my summer love's car stopped right behind us. In the summer time this is the girl I spend many days cruising the lake in her daddy's ski boat. We all rushed to hide the beer before realizing only my summer sweetheart was in the car. She had taken the day off from school in Massachusetts. She was visiting the bay to get away from life in Massachusetts for a day. I decided to skip hunting, because I could hunt any time! Today I would be with my girl. We walked a short distance across the beach to my friend's parents' cabin but once inside the cabin we decided it was too cold. We thought of a warm private place where we could spend the day together without being bothered. My parents were not home, so we could go to my house for the day. This could be the perfect setting for romance. To make it especially thrilling to be where my intentions were against the rules.

The day was perfect, with my father working and my mother visiting friends. Love was in the air, or at least my mind. Once in the house, we took a snack from the kitchen and went to my room on the second floor. Soft music and food relaxed us while we sat on the edge of the bed talking. The conversation was of events that happened during the months since we had seen each other in August. The time of day never crossed our mind since it was early. The mood was relaxed as we laid back and started making out. Relaxed and with full stomachs we fell asleep in each other's arms. Suddenly the door burst open, and my father started yelling, about how the Catholic religion condemns this. Shocked and mad, I started defending what had happened. My sweetheart left and our perfect day ended in disaster. My father grounded me because at seventeen he probably realized a whipping was not an option.

December came, and tension increased as I resisted conforming to family rules. I was in trouble in school for teasing girls. I was in trouble in town for raising Cain with my friends. Then I met the dream girl to get me through the winter. She was blonde beautiful and had her own car. This girl lived and worked in Massachusetts but had friends in Alton. This meant on most weekends she would drive to Alton for a visit. We became interest in each other on that first meeting and knew there would be more between us. A few weeks later we bumped into each other in town. I had no money and little gas in my car. I thought about how my parents were not home. The events that followed were almost a mirror image of the November scene with my summer sweetheart. My father sent both the girl and myself down the road while my mother cried attempting to maneuver around him. My father's departing words were "if you can't follow the rules of my house you can find your own house." At the same time my brothers and sister were in the up stairs bedroom windows waving good bye quietly so no one would hear them.

The day was late and dark. I decided to head south, so I stuck my thumb out and caught a ride. I made it to Manchester, New Hampshire, about 30 miles away. I arrived at about ten o'clock at night, I was cold and broke. I knew I was in trouble. I looked around and noticed a light in the Marine recruiter's office down the street. The sergeant was a friendly man who talked tough. I enjoyed talking with this man. Soon I just started telling this stranger my problems with my home life and school. I felt warm after a cup of coffee. The sergeant asked, "Where are you staying tonight?" I explained I had no idea where I would stay that night. I went on to explain it would be warm when I got to the southern states. The recruiter explained if I signed this paper, he could put me in a hotel for the night. I was quick to sign without even caring what it said. I was even more impressed when the sergeant informed me he would buy me breakfast in the morning.

The sergeant arrived at the hotel room at 5 o'clock in the morning, which was ok by me because I was up. My being out of bed and dressed surprised the sergeant. I explained I was raised on a farm. I always got up at this time to take care of the animals. We ate at a busy restaurant down the road. The Marine looked good in uniform: dress blues and a white hat. The Sergeant informed me that he would drive me to the airport in Boston, my flight left at 9 o'clock, and I would arrive in Parris Island by noon. The only questions I could ask were "Where" and "Why"? The sergeant didn't even miss a beat as he went on to explain everything. I would be in training, and this would make me a man. The training only lasted 90 days. I'd get a room and food, plus pay while I was there. The sergeant went on to explain that after I became a Marine, the Marine Corps would send me to school to work on aircraft. I was eager and excited by this time. When the sergeant explained I would travel around the world for free, I was on my way.

I arrived at Parris Island, South Carolina on a warm sunny December day. I watched my hair fall to the ground and thought to myself, what did I get into? The time up to this point was so full of men yelling at us that I did not have time to think. A minute later I was off to my new home as some man kept telling us he was our mother. This "mother" instructed us to call him sergeant. He quickly was immediately in my face telling me I was too small to be a Marine. The sergeant yelled from an inch away from my face, "I will make you beg to be quit. You're so small you're scum!"

I went through hell for the next few weeks as the drill sergeant tried to make me beg. I refused. The second morning I woke in what is referred to as the motivation platoon. This was a place designed to make or break recruits who the Drill Instructors thought were questionable Marine material. The reason I was assigned to this platoon came from my refusing to smile when ordered by the drill instructor. Weeks of marching, and crawling through the mud had taken a toll on the platoon. Boys were leaving one after another. Since tough training was not enough to make the rest of us quit it got worse. We started running dressed in full gear for five to ten miles at a time. The Drill Instructors would beat each recruit several times a day as a tool to discourage your continuation in the Marine Corps. The harsh conditions provoked a determination that increased as the training increased. The last ten of us would not beg. On a warm spring day I left Parris Island as a Marine private, heading for Camp Lejeune, North Carolina for infantry training.

The training was difficult. A harder part of being at Parris Island was the requirement for each recruit to write letters to their mother. In the first month of basic training the Drill Instructor kept a list of recruits who sent mail home. Near the end of the thirty days my name appeared on that list. I witnessed the lesson another recruit was given from the Drill Instructor for explaining his mother was dead. In the Drill Instructor's own words death is no excuse not to follow orders. The eye opening lesson could not be mistaken a Marine never questions an order.

Training at camp Lejeune was different than the weeks at Parris Island. We trained twelve hours a day and relaxed the other twelve hours. The instructors were not in our faces. If we did our job correctly, they left us alone. I finished my infantry training and was given orders to attend school at a naval air station in New Jersey. Having been promoted to private first-class, I was now a Marine heading for school.

The naval base in New Jersey seemed like a different life all together. I was now learning how to launch jet planes from an aircraft carrier and stop the same planes with a hook and rope. I was finished with the need to prove my resiliency. I was fascinated with the power of the Marine Corps, the machines, and everything around me. I became obsessed with learning every little thing about this new job. I started running six miles every morning to take up the time before class started. I found the running helped with my learning. I learned about the design of the equipment and the theory of vortex action (water spinning in opposite directions causing a breaking action). I could not fail and go home. This school lasted ninety days. I was so consumed with adventure it seemed like a day when it was over. I was a qualified Marine with thirty days leave to go back and strut as a Marine in a small New Hampshire town. The first day of summer arrived as I took my first step into the state of New Hampshire.

I arrived back in Alton, New Hampshire proud to be a Marine. I stood tall and invincible. I had been brain washed into thinking a Marine could do anything. The locals were not impressed. I guess the memory of my past was still on their minds. My friends in Alton still drank as popular way of spending their free time. This drinking routine was easy to fall back into for me. The demeaning attitude of the locals encouraged me to take the medicine to ease the painful reality of their rejection. The town folk were nice to me when I was present. They degraded me behind my back. I had thirty days. I fell into my old ways.

Now I had a pocket full of money and friends willing to help me spend it. It became the norm while I was home to just drink and party every night. I started what I thought would be a thirty-day party. The party ended abruptly in a friend's car late one night. This night stopped the fun. A large group of kids drank a lot of alcoholic beverages until the early hours of the next day. Two friends and I moved a large rock and several trees with another friend's car. The Chevy Vega was totaled and three young adults ended the night at the hospital.

The damage to my brain was massive. I was in a coma for days. The doctors had no hope. My eyes started to move on the eight day. My family's dreams and prayers were about to be answered. I had come back against the odds given by the medical staff. I opened my eyes as an infant in an eighteen-year-old's body. I woke up in the Portsmouth Naval Hospital in Portsmouth, New Hampshire. I met people who were introduced as my parents although I did not know what parents were any longer. The medical staff was astonished that I was even alive. The way I consumed knowledge over the next few weeks was inspiring to everyone. To grow mentally after such trauma to the brain was against the odds. I progressed during this time from the mental age of an infant, to some where around a ten-year-old developmentally. I lacked any understanding of responsibility or discipline but I was able to function as an infant.

I became aware of things around me and started talking and asking questions. Nobody would answer questions about me personally. The doctors advised not to since it could put me into shock if I learned about my past too fast. I had little understanding of the meaning of the answers but sometimes I would retain a memory of what was said. The more people talked the more I grasped the need to learn. My mind by this time was that of an inquisitive ten-year-old wanting to know as a child needs to learn in his young life. I liked talking to the retired Marine in the bed next to me because he would talk without fear of saying the wrong things to me.

This Marine had done twenty years in the corps. He fought in Vietnam twice on extended tours each time. The way this man loved to talk about the Marine Corps built my desire to be a fighting machine. Forty-five and retired made him pretty old for me to be friends with, but I was drawn to his wisdom. I learned what the Marine Corps meant from this man. I became filled with the hope of going to Vietnam to prove myself. The best thrill for a Marine was fighting in a war. Everybody kept telling me that I was a Marine. I believed that I needed to go to war. My progress mentally was in limbo between ten to twelve years for several weeks now. There was little hope I would improve.

The medical staff informed my parents and me that a medical discharge was being processed. In the next bed my Marine friend heard this discussion. After everyone left the room he advised me not to allow a medical discharge. In my eyes, this friend knew everything about the military. We spent the next few weeks signing out of our rooms for different hospital departments. We went to the basement and dressed in uniforms before going around the base. Each day we filled out forms requesting that I be transferred to Vietnam. This went on for a week, requesting change and transfer orders. Each form had to be placed in certain baskets in different departments. This Marine knew where to go and how to bluff people into believing he was in the proper place. He advised me to avoid certain departments that might reject the requests. The day of my discharge finally came. I spend the day checking off the base before I could pick up my orders. My parents could not understand how I received orders to El Toro, California. *I was now a Marine with no memory. I was on a path of adventure. My goal was to someday fight in the Vietnam War. The retired Marine and I were disappointed in my receiving orders to El Toro after all the effort in getting the transfer process completed. Our goal fell short but the medical discharge was changed that was the beginning. The*

Retired Marine explained how each time I checked into another base I could fill out a transfer request first. This would be a mission that makes me a Marine.

This Marine's parents had strong objections to my going back on active duty. I had no argument for going other than the defense that I was a Marine and I needed to go. I had no reason or memory that I could use to explain this to them. I had no idea what travel meant. I was like a child playing games. My father decided the Marine Corps might benefit my medical condition. The least it could do was guide my childish actions and teach me to take care of myself. To calm my mother's objections, he made me promise to write letters once a week. I agreed, although I did not know what a letter was. I didn't even know how to read or write.

Chapter Three: My First Assignment:

Marine Air Base El Toro California this was my first duty station as a Marine. Where was I going? What would I do? Would these people that called themselves my parents see me ever again? How would I get along without advice from the retired Marine?

These questions were answered when I remembered one of the last things this retired Marine told me "go do everything you can, travel, learn new jobs, have fun." On a very warm fall day I walked up to the main gate at Marine Air Base El Toro California in my civilian clothes. The Marine guard standing stiff at the main gate checked my identification card. After clearing security, I was directed to the administration unit of the base. I walked the short distance to the office even though it took me quite a long time because of the new and exciting events happening around me. My mind was distracted by all that was happening around me. I could see men with rifles marching up and down the streets. The jeeps and tanks plus all the other military equipment maneuvering in different areas. I knew this was going to be fun playing Army!

I finally reached the administration unit building. No one inside the office seemed capable of the least bit of friendliness. I was told to stand here, or to sit and wait. I was not asked to do anything except wait. Everybody acted like they were a boss the way commands were yelled at each other. After an hour of nothing I started filling out forms. I started the paperwork in the room that I first entered. The number of questions I asked because I didn't understand the meaning of the forms I had to fill out. This irritated the administrative Marines. The accident in Alton New Hampshire left me with the mind of a ten-year-old even though to others I appeared a bit stupid but normal. I then was directed down a long hallway and told to check in at each door. The process was the same at each door. I knocked and was told to wait. Sometimes the wait was only a few minutes. Other time I waited over an hour. At the end of the hall I was told to wait outside for a jeep to take me to my unit.

The jeep that was to transport me arrived a short time later. The driver loaded my duffel bag in the back. I was finally finished with the paperwork part of this day. Riding in a jeep was great. The driver was a friendly person who talked freely to me. He was a member of the motor pool assigned as a driver for the Marine Air Base Squadron (MABS) on the runway. All he did during the day is drive other Marines around the base in a jeep. I told him I hoped I could get a job driving a jeep. That is when the driver explained what my M.O.S. 7011 stood for (Military Occupation Service, Launch and Recovery). The job sounded even better: shooting planes up in to the air off elastic cable and stopping planes with a hook. The driver described my job as "the same as they do on an Air Craft Carrier only on land. I did not understand, but I couldn't wait to get started.

My face was all smiles when the jeep pulled up to the MABS unit building. It was located on the flight line, next to the runway. The driver told me to leave my bag in the jeep. I was only at this building for my barracks assignment. Once inside the building I met a lot of men who were happy to see me. The unit was short handed and had been for a while. They were looking forward to having a new man to help with the work. The accident left me with a short memory so as I met the men I could not remember their names. The smile was still on my face as the driver took me to my new home. This was an active Marine Air Base and I was now playing Marine. A squadron such as this could be ordered to pack up and trade places with a squadron in Vietnam at any time. The two Squadrons are required to complete the transfer with each other within seventy-two hours with no advanced notice. As the driver explained this the excitement of going to Vietnam filled my head with anticipation

I was excited at 0500 hours the next morning when I woke up. My new home was a four story new concrete building. I lived in a two-man room on the second floor. The room was twelve feet by twelve feet with two built-in wall lockers. There were two desks next to the bunk beds on one side of the room. I took the top bunk because the bottom bunk was prepared neatly with the blanket tight fitted and the pillow positioned perfectly. The room shone with cleanliness. Before I started my day, I cleaned the room and made my bed before I left for the mess hall. My roommate's bunk was not slept in, but that didn't matter to me. I just wanted to get to my new job and shoot planes into the air.

I arrived at the MABS unit for my first day of work. The excitement changed to desperation when I was assigned to cleaning the floor. The job was far from launching planes. But the experience of being on a Marine base near the runway kept the excitement alive. I swept the floor from one side of the workshop to the other. I moved everything I could in order to get every spec of dirt. I even had others help me if something was too big or heavy. This job gave me a reason to touch and look at things I had no idea what they were. Just touching these powerful items was a little boy's dream. Well into my third hour of sweeping the floor a corporal stopped me. He suggested anyone who gets this excited over sweeping a floor is nuts.

I was now assigned to help a Sergeant dissemble an Absorber. The rubber liner needed to be replaced for some reason. Seeing as I was straight from training this work would all be fresh in my mind, so they thought. We started work as the Sergeant had a crane operator from the motor pool hoist out the center of the tub. The Sergeant told me to get him a half-inch wrench to remove a bolt. He got quite upset when I asked him, "what is a wrench? The remainder of the day went much the same, others not understanding I had no memory of life's normal happenings, the Sergeant having to explain everything he told me to do. It was clear that by the end of the first day that I had no idea of what to do. I was transferred to the MABS armory the next morning.

I was still a part of the same MAG (Marine Air Group) and MABS unit, but not on the runway. I was ordered not to report for work the next day. Orders would be delivered to me at the barracks, they said. I still got up at 0500 hours the next morning. Unpacking my bag and making my wall locker neat took quite some time. The mess hall was next on my list. There was time in this day to look at things as I walked down the barracks hallway. The floors, walls, even the handles on the doors shone. This had to be the cleanest hotel around. A Corporal stopped me at the end of the hall and asked, "Are you PFC Macdonald." I responded "Yes sir," as he handed me my orders to report to the MAG Armory. He made a comment to me that he was enlisted, not an officer, so I shouldn't call him sir. I had to ask, "what is an armory?" The Corporal looked at me with a crazed expression and walked away. I met some guys who lived in my barracks at the mess hall that morning. They were interesting to talk to about everything. I got directions from them on how to find the Armory. I still had no idea what the Armory did.

My job as a squadron Armor began that morning when I reported. I stood in front of the Armory Officer and reported to work. The questions in my mind were asking me, "How?" or "What will I do here?" The Lieutenant walked me down a long hallway. There were jailhouse doors on both sides every fifty feet. To identify the unit, above each door was a sign stating the unit that Armory belongs too. The last door on the left we stopped at and the Lieutenant took out a key. "This door is to be locked at all times except when you enter or leave," the Lieutenant said. The Lieutenant went on to explain as we entered the room that there were over three thousand weapons in this unit alone. My job was to take each weapon apart. I was to inspect each weapon for proper operation or defects. I was to repair any damage and put all weapons together in perfect condition. The Lieutenant continued, saying each serial number is to be logged in the book. A check mark was to be placed next to the correct serial number on the unit inventory sheet. After all this was completed, I was to clean the unit room for inspection. I thought, Wow this is great being with all these different types of weapons!" As far as I was concerned, I had never seen some of these weapons before. I soon learned in the Marine Corps it doesn't matter if you know something or not. The Lieutenant was getting irrate with my questions. He started answering me with the phrase before each answer "You should know that." I was then given a special identification card to trade the guard at the Armory door each day for the key to get in my unit. My last question made the Lieutenant mad. I asked "Could I keep any extra weapons I found in the unit?" He responded in a loud voice, "There better not be. If there are, get rid of them". I had a job to do. I learned how to disassemble, clean, and reassemble each weapon. The process was fun but I kept forgetting the order the parts went back together. The mechanics just came to me as I worked. The more I repeated the process, the more things fell into place.

A cloud of bewilderment came over me on the first day. I stood in the large room with stacks of boxes and racks of rifles, with no thought of what to do. I eventually started moving things around to look at what was there. Doing this created a small work area. I was amazed and excited at the time to be in a room with all these military toys. The M-16 came apart easily on the top of a large box I used as a workbench. I cleaned, and polished each individual part before placing it back on the rifle frame. The order the parts as they went back together got confusing, but the more I did the faster I worked and the less mistakes I made. The M-14 I had trouble with. After doing so many M-16 rifles I couldn't adjust the order of the parts to reassemble an M-14 efficiently. I learned my job well over the next several weeks. I reported for work every morning at 0630 hours straight from the mess hall.

The next step after the cleaning and reassemble was finished is to check the serial number of each weapon. The first part was to write each number on my log sheet. Then I checked the units inventory sheet and make a check mark after the number. The rifles were placed on the racks in numerical sequence. The racks were stacked in the rows of the MABS unit armory in numerical order of the racks. I cleaned and polished each section of the room before the area was filled. I completely finished all the rifles and was now starting on grenade launchers, bazookas and law (light antitank weapon). These weapons came in metal boxes so cleaning was not so hard. The metal boxes were airtight containers so the elements couldn't effect them.

The only thing left was the M-50 machine guns. I cleaned ten of these weapons and with each one I pretended I was fighting the enemy. The time had come to check off the numbers on the unit inventory sheet. There was one extra M-50 machine gun that had no matching numbers.

This was great. The Lieutenant said I should get rid of any weapon not on the list. I took the weapon back to the barracks right past the guard at the armory door. He never checked anyone going out except to trade badges for keys. I thought I was following orders; carrying the M-50 in its box. I walked past the guard. "Since my car accident, I took everything people said quite literally. I didn't have any idea this could get me in trouble." Once back in the barracks, I needed to think of how to mail it home. I didn't figure there was any rush. Money was the question. How much would I need?

I liked my job because I was learning a lot about weapons. The base was becoming less confusing to me each day. My inventory and organizing was almost complete at the Armory. I was meeting and talking to a lot of different people each day. My roommate showed up at our room and I got to talk with him. He lived with his wife off base and only came to the room to clean it every other week. I liked being a Marine and I was learning new things each moment.

I received orders from the Corporal at the barracks duty desk one morning. The orders said to report to the Captain's office of the MABS unit by 0900 hours. Having no idea what I was reporting for, I went to chow. The day seemed normal as I walked in to the building containing the Captain's office. I took a seat in front of the Captain's door to wait. I tried always to get to appointments early because sometimes I forgot for a few minutes where I was going. Being early gave me time to get where I belonged when my brain remembered where to go. I was used to waiting, as are most Marines. The fact is no matter how early a Marine gets some place, it seems the Marine that you are reporting too is always late. My reporting this time showed me why it was important to be early.

At 0900 hours exactly the Captain walked up to me. I snapped to attention. "PFC Macdonald reporting as ordered, Sir" I said. The Captain in a direct commanding voice ordered me to follow him into his office. I followed him in and stood at attention at the center front of his desk. I heard the door bang shut behind me. Not expecting I had done anything wrong my mood was relaxed while still at attention. The Captain in a matter of seconds was in my face yelling, "How did you get a job that should have taken eight months done in eight days?" I was confused: what job? What should take eight months? My head was spinning questions with no answers. I finally stated "Sir, I did my job as ordered." The Captain never flexed a muscle in his face. Looking me straight in the eyes, the words snapped out from only the movement of his lower lip, "You would have to work day and night to get this job done in this small amount of time". (He commanded). My response to the Captain was to assure him I did work day and night, "Yes sir". The Captain then informed me that the MABS Armory unit better be perfect on inspection. He picked up the phone and ordered the Lieutenant to meet us at the Armory in five minutes. The meeting ended as I followed the Captain out of the office.

The Lieutenant who gave me the orders to clean and inventory was at the Armory door waiting. The Captain was surprised when his superior (the Major) met us as we walked up the long hallway. The Captain and Major talked while we walked, but I could not hear what was said. The Lieutenant snapped to attention as we approached. The Major as we neared the door informed everyone he would inspect this unit himself. Asking for an inventory sheet the Major walked through the cell door as the Lieutenant opened it. Handing the Major a clipboard with papers on it the Captain passed by the Lieutenant staying one step behind the Major. The Lieutenant ordered me to guard the door as he followed the others in.

I read the words on the clipboard as it passed by me. The one inch red letters stamped on the top of the page said "Shipment Document". The three officers took several minutes going through the armory unit. Then the Major clasped his hands behind his back. He then slowly turned back toward the door with his eyes surveying every box and rack in the room. Words started to break the silence dominating the room. "This is the finest job I have ever seen, who is responsible?" commanded the Major. All eyes turned toward a scared Marine at attention guarding a door. "PFC Macdonald," the Lieutenant stated. The Major then removed a weapon from a rack and positioned himself not two feet away from me. Holding the weapon in one hand he removed the bolt assembly. "Is every weapon this clean, soldier?" the Major asked. In a clear strong voice I stated "Sir, yes sir, I dissembled, repaired, cleaned, polished, and logged every weapon sir." "PFC Macdonald did every weapon's serial number appear on the log sheet?" the Major asked. "No sir," I responded, "I removed the extra M-50 as the Lieutenant ordered, sir." The Major (as he handed the clipboard back to the captain) ordered a report on his desk by noon.

My job title was still MABS Armor, but I was ordered to my barracks until further orders. I had no sooner walked back to my barracks than the Lieutenant arrived with two Military Police men. I was asked if I had an M-50 machine gun in my room. I took the M-50 out of my wall locker and gave it to one of the MP's. The Lieutenant appeared quite angry. I stood at attention next to my open wall locker. The Lieutenant went crazy yelling at me. He used all kinds of names and words describing where I was going. The Lieutenant left as the MP's informed me I was restricted to the barracks. I could leave for necessary things like chow, running, etc. I was further told I was waiting disciplinary action. The words meant nothing to me. I was confused. I just listened.

The Lieutenant came back into the room as the MP's finished describing what I could not do while awaiting disciplinary action. The Lieutenant ordered the MP's to remove the M-50 and leave. The Lieutenant was much more relaxed now as he asked me "Do you know what you did?" Without waiting for an answer he continued, "How could you do something so stupid?" I was in a state of confusion, and blurted out "What is a disciplinary action sir?" The Lieutenant explained I was in trouble. Removing a weapon from the Armory is wrong. He went on to explain I would be lucky to just lose stripes, (this is a form of military demotion in rank or pay grade) but I would most likely go to the brig, which is a military prison.

Barracks restriction was not bad for me. The first day was difficult just trying to remember to tell the duty NCO every time I left the barracks. My roommate Dave came by on the first day. He was curious why I was on barracks restriction, so we sat down and talked. We talked about everything from his wife to my dropping out of school and joining the Marine Corps. His wife Linda was a teacher at a local elementary school in Garden Grove, a city about ten miles from the base. He talked about how he was going to college after work three nights a week. Someday he hoped to work as a teacher. Education was the most important thing to compete in life, Dave told me. The point he seemed to be making was telling me to go to school. He went on to tell me with all my free time on barracks restriction I should go over to the Marine Education Counselor's office and see about getting my high school diploma. Dave even gave me directions to get to the education building. Learning is important to me, I kept thinking. Learn as much as you can. I decided to go and find out more about education.

The Marine Education Counselor was a civilian lady who worked on the base. She was pleasant to talk with. I felt comfortable as she explained how I could take a course through the mail to get my high school diploma. The Marine Corps would pay for the course as long as I completed it. She would arrange with my local high school back in Alton, New

Hampshire to take courses so I could graduate from Alton once I had enough credit. But I wanted to learn now, not in a couple months after we heard from Alton about which courses I needed. The counselor asked if I wrote letters to family or friends. I informed her I had promised I would, but didn't know how. I never explained about my amnesia because I still was not aware that I was different because of the injuries from the accident. She suggested I take an English course called Letter Writing. The counselor thought my high school would accept English credits toward my diploma. She gave me some books and explained what to do.

The course was interesting. I read a few pages in the book, then I did a multiple-choice paper that would separate the sections of the book. I learned in writing letters how to make a sentence. I could take a group of sentences and make paragraphs. The purpose was to group ideas together. I started practicing writing letters to my parents. The course was a great way to spend a few minutes here or there when I had free time. I found that if I spent any more than a few minutes, I got a headache and felt confused. I worked with the English course while on barracks restriction to occupy my idle time.

The second day I started running to keep in shape and occupy time. I ran about six miles before chow each morning. I always woke up about 0500 hours. The mess hall was open from 0600 to 0830 for breakfast. I thought if I run from 0530 to 0630 then take a shower. I could avoid the crowds at the mess hall. After chow, I was just hanging around the barracks watching television in the lobby. Another Marine was cleaning the area so I helped him with that job. I learned that for one week at a time everyone who lives in the barracks gets this detail. I enjoyed working at the barracks because if something broke I would just fix it. The floor wax buffer broke. I took the worn brushes off the armature (of the motor) and reversed them. The buffer worked fine after that. I fixed desk drawers, legs to chairs, doors and knobs. The list never ended. I forgot all about my discipline hearing and started believing that I worked in the barracks. I had been on barracks restriction for two weeks when the orders came for me to appear at the MABS Captain's office.

I reported to the Captain's office fifteen minutes early and took a seat. The Captain's door opened at exactly 0910 hours for my disciplinary hearing. I marched into his office and stood at attention at the front center of his desk. The Captain kept asking me question after question. He did not give me any time to answer. I could only remember the last question asked. I was becoming so confused that when the Captain requested an answer I was lost. I started to talk but I couldn't remember what I wanted to say. I was lost. The Captain was right in my face. He was yelling "You have to be the stupidest but most efficient Marine in the world." The Captain went on to explain how the Major was impressed with the MABS unit. The Major wanted to know why a Captain worked an enlisted man twenty-hour days. The Major did not seem too happy, the Captain stated.

The charges were dropped against me. I had little understanding what was happening around me. The effects of the injuries from the accident still left my mental awareness at the level of a ten year old. I was accepting this adventure as a learning experience. The thought of the retired Marine back at the Portsmouth Naval Hospital kept appearing in my thoughts during this day, "accept what happens, but learn every job you can and the stripes will come back". I did not lose any stripes, but I was too lost in thought to be relieved.

Chapter Four: El Toro Guard Duty

The administration officer ordered me back to the barracks to await my next duty assignment. The restrictions that had been on me were lifted which meant I could do what I wanted without checking in with anyone. I calmly walked back to the barracks enjoying the surroundings without a care in the world. What had happened at my disciplinary hearing didn't seem real. It was like a dream. A story in an adventure book. I was a squadron armor. I wasn't a squadron armor. I was in trouble. I wasn't in trouble. I could remember some things, other things I would forget seconds after they happen. By the time I arrived back at the barracks, the only part of what happen that I could remember is the charges were dropped. The main talk going on around the barracks that day was, how much time in the brig will Macdonald get? I knew or was friends with almost all three hundred Marines in the barracks. Everybody I saw would ask me questions about the disciplinary action. My answer was "the charges were dropped" There was no other answer, for I knew nothing else. I could not say anymore because my mind did not retain any more information pertaining to the action. I went back to my job of working around the barracks, believing in my mind that I had always worked there.

The administration office within a few days ordered me to report for base guard duty. My orders told me to report to the Sergeant of the guard at 1600 hours the next day. The first thing I had to do was find where the guard building was located. I left early the afternoon of my new job from the barracks because I didn't know how long a walk the other side of the base would take. I found the building located in the middle of no where. The building was lime green about twenty-four feet wide, sixty feet long. The trees were cut back about one hundred feet from around the building with a tarred parking area near the door. A radio antenna was at the edge of the woods extended high into the air.

I walked into the front room of the building to report to work. The top of the desk just as you enter the room was about six feet off the floor. It extended twenty-four feet across the room from wall to wall. A Marine in full work uniform looked down on the entrance with cold eyes. "Yes may I help you?" The guard asks. "PFC Macdonald reporting for guard duty as ordered." I replied. The guard looked at me funny and asked How did you get out here? He then explained that the jeep just left to pick me up at the barracks. The guard picked up a radio and told someone to forget the barracks pickup. The next step came when the guard gave me forms to fill out.

The Sergeant came from the back room to give me further instructions on my new assignment. I would be going on a roving patrol of the ammo bunkers staged around the base. I would work from 1700 hours at night to 0600 hours the next day. Four days of work then two days off. In the event of an alert my shifts are seven days and I would live out of the bunkroom. Each time I came on duty I would be issued a 45-calaber side arm and M-16 rifle with ammo. The Sergeant warned me that every round of ammo used needed a full report filled out: "So don't fire any." The Sergeant said. I would be riding with another Marine for my first two weeks. In this time I had to learn the routes, check in points and times. I also had to get my military jeep license issued.

I knew I would like this job driving a jeep all over the place. We started on our patrol at exactly 1700 hours. The ammo bunkers were piles of dirt sixty, to seventy feet in the air. Located on opposite sides of the piles were concrete boxes extending out. These boxes had metal doors with bars and chains to hold them shut. These doors lead to a large room under the dirt where the Marine Corps stored its bombs. There were thirty bunkers staged at different location around the base. Some of the bunkers were located near or between buildings. Other bunkers were located in remote areas of the base. Either way, you had to know where to go because with the trees and bushes they looked like natural landscape.

The remote bunkers seemed to be the ones the drivers liked best. You drive the jeep down these curved dirt roads deep into the woods. It's kind of scary because it is so dark. All you can see is what the headlights shine on. Branches hang down and sometimes brush against the windshield. Other branches extend out from the side and slap you in the face when you not paying attention. The bumps are the best part of these roads. The drivers have every bump location printed in their brains.

A jeep is a metal box with wheels that go any place that the driver dares to go. These vehicles where not made for comfort, just fun. The seats are canvas-covered metal frame with no seat belts. A small bump just bangs your butt real hard. The big bumps can lift you out of your seat. The drivers like to initiate new guards by testing how high out of the seat they can bump you. It being my first night, I had no idea what to expect. We were riding down this dirt road at an increasing speed. I had my left hand holding the M-16 rifle between the seats. The guards carried a loaded rifle (magazine loaded, chamber emptied) in the jeep. They also carried a loaded 45-caliber in a holster on their side. My right hand was resting on my right knee. I was relaxed enjoying my new job. The driver got this slight smile on his face. Then all of a sudden the jeep hit a bump. My butt went above the height of the windshield. My right hand reached out and clamped onto the top rail of the windshield. The M-16 never escaped the grip of my left hand. When the jeep stopped a short distance latter my left foot was behind the seat I had been sitting in. My right foot was in my seat. I was up against the windshield with my head over the top of it. The driver in total amazement sat with one hand holding the steering wheel. His other hand was on the stock of the rifle. He was squealing the words nobody will believe this one. I started laughing, wanting to do it again.

The time now was getting to be around 0100 hours. We were in a remote area as the driver checked the bunker doors. After that stop was completed the driver took a left off the road between some trees. Straight up this steep hill to a clearing at the top. The driver explained to me that it was now naptime. I was too excited to sleep. I watched the driver set the timer on his alarm then put his head back and closed his eyes. I got out of the jeep and started walking around looking at different things. The night was dark but up this high, the lights off in a distance could be seen 360 degrees. It looked like we were the eye of a sunflower. Off in a distance I could see an airplane on final approach. I imagined the base was under attack and pretended to fight the enemy off. Then behind me this strange noise caught my ear. I dropped to my knees thinking the enemy had over run our position. I would spring up and surprise them. It was just the driver. He shut his alarm off and told me to get into the jeep. The time had come to start our patrol again.

The race was on. We had to get to the next checkpoint to log in at the correct time. I thought maybe that the driver had overslept. I placed the rifle between my legs to hold it with my knees. My hands were down by my sides holding the seat tight to my butt. The jeep was weaving between trees at a high speed. We were hitting bumps so hard I thought maybe the jeeps wheels might touch the ground long enough to hit the next bump but not much more. Up and down, back and forth the driver was spinning the steering wheel, shifting to a higher gear then lower gear, pressing on the brake, the clutch, the throttle, all this at a crazy speed. Finally we stopped to check in at the guard shack. I looked at the driver as if to ask why didn't we leave a little sooner? Without my saying a word the driver stated, It's a game; I sleep one minute longer each night to see if I can make it here on time. We walked into the shack together.

I was finishing up with my last night of training and the next day I was scheduled to take my driver's test. This was a military certification test to drive a jeep. I was assigned to ride with a private as my driver, this night. A private (I thought to myself)--this guy looks like an old man. He must be at least thirty-nine years old. I found out later on that he was thirty-six with nineteen years active duty. He was a gunny sergeant up until last year, which is when he got busted for drinking on duty. The punishment he received was to be a private for his last two years. On his last day of service before retiring he gets his stripes back, provided he doesn't get into any trouble.

The night started out as a normal one. We drove around checking the doors on bunkers one after another. Dark was starting to set in; it was an hour or so past sunset. We headed down the back roads to the remote bunkers. I knew most of the roads out here. I at least knew which roads went to the bunkers. But the private took a route that I had never been on. He drove at a high speed like it was the in thing to do. One hand on the wheel and his left foot propped up on the doorframe. He casually drove this way into the night. He was talking asking me questions like as if he was pumping me for information. I was telling him how this was my last night and that tomorrow I take the drivers test. The private asked if I had qualified at jumping jeeps yet. I had no idea so in a confident voice I said, Not yet but I hope to.

To qualify to jump jeeps did man ever encounter one of the most exciting events! The private and I checked out the rest of the bunkers, and then completed our 0100-hour check in with the Sergeant of the Guard. The night was much of the same as a normal guard duty, except we were in a rush, never stopping for our regular brakes. We were back in the remote area near bunker six. The path up the south side was thick with brush and trees. There was a worn tire path straight up to the top. The north side of the hill was mostly grass and small bushes, all the way from top to the bottom. I knew the landscape of this area quite well because it was one of the nap areas.

The private drove to the edge of the path to go to the top. He turned the jeep in the opposite direction and drove about one half-mile straight across the field. We came to a complete stop. The driver turned the jeep to point back at the bunker. The private suggested I put the rifle under the emergency brake handle to keep it from leaving. I had just finished letting the brake handle down on the rifle when the jeep started racing toward the bunker. We were going fast enough to be in fourth gear at the beginning of the upward path. The private down shifted as the jeep slowed because of the steep ness of the hill. We crested the top in second gear. We were traveling at close to forty miles per hour. The private looked at me and stated, "Hold on--this is what I do when I am bored." The jeep wheels left the ground as we flew off the other side of the bunker. The jeep bounced a few times when the wheels landed about halfway down the hill. With both hands clutched to the steering wheel the driver stopped about fifty yards from the bunker. The private was the one shocked. He thought I would be scared but the smile on my face said something different. I was so excited I asked him to do it again.

The private still holing the steering wheel with both hands agreed maybe one more time. He wanted to check a few bunkers first before we jumped. The private after a while took one hand of the steering wheel and placed his foot on the doorframe. He started talking about how that jump must have been a record. "Nobody could ever jump that good," he assured me. I asked the private about qualifying for jumping jeeps. He explained how guards did this to learn how the jeep handles in a tough situation. This was a secret test conducted among the guards only, and we never tell anyone else the private explained.

Our second jump was started with about thirty minutes left on the shift. The private stopped the jeep about the same distance from the bunker and got out. He told me to drive the jeep on this jump. I was eager so I hoped across the seat in a flash. I started up the hill, at a speed, which seemed fast to me. The private must not have thought so, because he kept yelling, "go faster". I crested the top at maybe twenty miles per hour but I thought I was going 100 miles per hour. At least it felt I was traveling that fast. The jeep wheels probably never left the ground. I held the steering wheel with both hands. My breath going in and out as fast as a jet engine could push it. We landed (if we ever left) and I stopped at the bottom of the bunker. My stomach was in my head as I looked at the private. The private smiled and said, "You will learn." We changed positions and headed to the barracks to pick up the next shift.

This was the start of two days off for me. Before I could do anything else, I needed to get my military license certification. I was off to the motor pool building for my testing. The driver part would be easy I thought to myself, but how would I do on the written test? I had read the eleven-page book every day for the last two weeks, but I could not remember a word in the book. I sat down and looked at the test. There were fifty multiple-choice questions. My mind was a blank. I sat looking at the questions and answers for fifty-five minutes. A voice that yelled from another room said five minutes left. I just started checking off boxes in the answer page. A Corporal who lived in my barracks entered the room and sat down at the desk. "Line up single file in front of my desk," the Corporal said. The ten of us stood in line while the Corporal placed a piece of cardboard over the answer sheet and called a number out. A private sitting at another table wrote the number down. You needed forty-out of fifty correct to pass. After your test was corrected, if you passed, it was more waiting in the next room. I was the last Marine in the line. I handed my answer sheet over to the Corporal. He placed the cardboard over my answer sheet. I could see none of my answers were correct. The Corporal yelled fifty and folded the answer sheet up and placed it in his pocket. I just walked in the other room and took a seat.

In this room the clerk would take your picture for the license. You waited until it was developed then you go to get the Corporal to stamp your driver's classification on the license form before they sealed it in plastic.

I was only here to get my jeep classification stamp. My turn came last at the Corporal's desk. I sat down and watched the Corporal stamp jeep, duce and a half, crane, and forklift on my license. I looked bewildered as the Corporal said, "thanks for fixing my desk chair in the barracks last month." It was now time for southern California to meet me.

I had found a ten speed bike in the trash dumpster a few weeks earlier. The frame was bent as if someone had driven over it with a car. The tubes that connected the seat rear wheel section to the front steering section were bent so the bike formed a V shape. I cut the bent tubes with a hacksaw I borrowed. The base had a hobby shop with all kinds of tools they let you use for free. I took some solid medal round bars out of the waste pile near the hobby shop. I rammed the medal bars into the bike tubes to hook the front part to the back part of the bike. I then took duct tape and wrapped it around and around the fixed area. This would clamp the tubes to the bars plus cover up the mess. The bike looked brand new except for the duct tape. And it worked, which was all I cared about.

I left the base after I took a shower and put civilian clothes on. I had only a few dollars to spend but I wanted to see southern California, so why not I thought. My mission was to ride to the entrance to

Disneyland. I heard everyone talking about how close it was so I got directions and was off. The description of the freeway sounded like it would be a good road to take. Just as I started down my first freeway a cop stopped in front of me. He informed me that I needed to use a different road; freeways were for vehicles only. The short trip now would take the entire day to reach the Mickey Mouse standing at the entrance of Disneyland. The traffic and number of people were mind numbing to me. Southern California was one packed place to live, I thought. Finally reaching Disneyland, standing at the entrance felt good to me. I wasn't going to go in Disneyland, because I did not have the money to waste. My goal was to reach the entrance and go to Dave and Linda's house for dinner.

I had directions from Disney Land to Dave's house, which happened to be halfway back to the base. I surprised myself with the directions, when in less than an hour I was at their door. Dave had just gotten home from work. I parked my bike as Dave was getting out of his car. I met Linda when we entered the house. She was a beautiful woman, I thought as I shook her hand. We had a great meal, then sat around and talked into the early hours. I woke up on their couch when I heard Dave in the other room getting dressed for work. We put my bike in Dave's car trunk, so I could ride with him back to the base. I spent that day writing letters and sleeping.

I thought all night about how crowded California was and why they called roads freeways out here. The day had arrived for solo patrols in my own jeep. Everything else got swept out of my mind when I woke up that day. By 1400 hours I was eager to get to work so I got in my utility (work) uniform and started sitting around waiting for the 1700 hour pick up. Eventually I started walking out to the guard shack. I think the time was 1600 hours: why wait I thought? I was about half way to the guard shack when the roving patrol jeep stopped beside me. The Lance Corporal driving asked if I was headed out to the guard shack and was I the Armor? I thought back and remembered I once worked in an Armory. I said "yes". The guard then explained how he dropped his rifle (that is a major offence for a Marine to show disrespect for his rifle) and got mud in the chamber. He went on with how he took it apart on the top of a bunker to clean it. The firing pin dropped out of the jeep onto the ground. He got out of the jeep and stepped on it. The pin was bent and would not fit in the bolt action hole. The guard wanted to know if I would fix it for him. I agreed, but told him that I was on my way to work. I could do it tomorrow if that was ok. He advised me that if I worked on it now he would work my shift until it was done. I jumped in the jeep for a ride the rest of the way out to the guard shack. Once at the guard shack I signed in and got my weapons issued to me. I met the Lance Corporal back out at the jeep and traded rifles with him. Off he went riding around in the jeep on my patrol. I went into the bunkroom to repair and clean his rifle.

The Lance Corporal gave me a three inch silver nail like item along with his rifle. I had no idea what the item was but maybe I would recognize where it went later as I worked on the rifle. Once in the bunkroom I set up a little work area and took the rifle apart. I could remember bits and pieces of the process as I dissembled the rifle. The procedure just seemed to come back to me the more I worked on the rifle. I completely dissembled the weapon and started cleaning and polishing each piece. I cleaned dirt and mud out of the barrel then shined it clean. Everything to do with the rifle came back to me as if I was sitting in the armory cage working as in the past. I did not know the names of the separate parts but I knew where they belonged. I had the entire rifle finished and back together in less than an hour. The rifle would not fire. I had tried to straighten the slight bend in the firing pin but the firing pin just wouldn't work once back in the rifle. I would have to try something else, I thought to myself as I started to dissemble the rifle again.

I was just sitting back looking at an empty coat hanger on the wall. My mind started to dream of how you could wrap that around someone's neck as a weapon. Maybe you could hook it on something to climb out a window. If you cut a piece off it you could put a handle on it for a knife to defend yourself. Hey why not cut a piece off it? You could cut a firing pin out of it. The metal would be soft enough to shape but strong enough to click when you pull the trigger. I got the coat hanger and cut a piece the same size as the firing pin. The next two hours I spent filing the coat hanger with the finger nail file that was on my pocketknife. I shaped the new firing pin to the exact size and shape as the old one. The new pin was the greenish brown color of the coat hanger, not the silver color as a normal firing pin. The rifle clicked when you pulled the trigger, so why would the color matter, I thought. The rifle was so clean and polished the Sergeant of the guard would probably just glance at it before sticking in the rack go back to the armory.

I heard the jeep with the Lance Corporal pull up to the rear door. We exchanged weapons then I went back through the building to the Guard desk. I had asked the sergeant earlier to let the Lance Corporal to do a couple hours of my shift and I would do a couple hours of his so he could come in late the next day. The Lance Corporal told the Sergeant of the guard his wife had a doctor's appointment first thing in the morning. She was pregnant, so no one questioned that excuse. The next day the Lance Corporal would come in on time so I didn't do extra duty and if needed he could just say the appointment was canceled.

The time was for my 0100-hour rounds to begin on patrol. This was to be my first solo patrol. I was excited but there was the unique mystery of doing guard duty alone. The feeling a child gets when a parent show adult trust during those times before maturity. The new things I learned each night kept my interest growing to want more. There were simple things like if you turn the knob on the top of the gearshift it comes off. Then there were difficult jobs such as fixing a broken jeep in an isolated area. I was now a Marine Guard and I wanted to learn everything I could about this job.

I did at first have trouble learning how to travel over the bunkers at high speed. The old private told me, "It's something every Marine should know" It was important for every Marine to know how to handle a jeep when its wheels leave the ground. Slowly I started jumping a jeep off the bunkers. Each night I would go over the bunker at least one time. The first night my speed couldn't have been over twenty miles per hour. I started up the hill not even caring about the consequences if I crashed. I was a Marine; nothing could hurt me. I crested the top of the bunker. My stomach went straight to my head. It felt like when an elevator drops too fast. I clenched the steering wheel with both hands. I felt to myself like this was the best jump anyone has ever done. The jeep speed had increased when I reached the bottom of the bunker. The jeep's wheels probably never left the ground, combined with my not taking my foot off the throttle helped increase the speed. The jeep going down hill accelerating added to the excitement of my first jump. I increased the speed of the jeep five-miles per hour per jump. I soon was above the forty miles per hour of the old private's jumps.

The maximum speed of a jeep was sixty-six miles per hour, I found out. A jeep traveling sixty six-miles per hour would fly about two hundred or more feet in the air. The only trouble is, after two jumps the rear suspension would fail. To do two jumps a night would be unusual but sometimes it did occur. This meant at least one jeep a week was failing at some point during use. The rear coil or leaf springs would in the next day or so, while being driven by motor pool personnel, break. The guard shack very seldom drove the same jeep in one week's time. The day shift at the start of shift was delivered at 0900 hours a clean refueled jeep by the motor pool. The source of damage to the jeeps was unknown. That is why the Sergeant of the Guard only requested we slow up when going over bumps. The motor pool was investigating speed traveled by guard personnel. The officer in charge of the guard unit did not want the blame to fall on him. So the orders came down to the Sergeant of the guard to make sure the damage did not happen because of the guard unit. I followed the Sergeant's order to slow down. I slowed down even though it made my bunker inspection time increase. The need for a Marine driver to know how a jeep reacts when its wheels leave the ground was training and must be continued.

The jumping was normal routine for every Marine as a learning tool, I thought. Iit could not be the problem that everyone was discussing that might be causing the damage.

The shift was almost over when I approached my favorite bunker to jump. My jumps for several weeks were at the maximum speed the jeep would accelerate to. I started at the normal spot about a half-mile from the base of the bunker. I found that if I could get up to sixty-six miles per hour before starting up, I would hold my speed better. When the wheels start up the hill I would down shift into third gear. The engine would be racing at high Rpm's but this way the jeep wouldn't lose speed. I would still be traveling at sixty six-miles per hour when I left the top of the bunker. The rifle was placed under the brake handle to keep it in the jeep with me and off I went. I was about to fly!

The full moon shone over the top of the bunker lighting the area. The jeep was sounding good; the engine roared as I started my climb. I could feel this was going to be my best jump ever. I crested the top of the bunker and the jeep's wheels left the ground. I leaned back in my seat holding the steering wheel with both hands in a relaxed type grip. I could see I was above the treetops as the bunker below me sank sharply down hill. The glory of knowing I was a Marine made me feel proud. This jump would never be beaten.

I could feel the jeep was about to land. I tightened my grip on the steering wheel. I was ready but a bit overexcited with what I had done. Just as the jeep's wheels were about to touch the ground I heard the Sergeant of the Guard's voice scream "Attention!" I glanced to my left straight into the Sergeant of the Guards eyes as I felt the jeep wheels touch the ground. This Marine (the sergeant of the guard) did not move a muscle as the jeep landed five feet in front of him. The speed and forward motion caused the jeep to travel a distance before I could safely stop it. The Sergeant was right in my face before I could get out of the jeep. Then the Sergeant drove back to the guard shack as he informed me I was in trouble. Once at the guard shack I was assigned to desk duty. This desk duty was for the remainder of my shift and more time was added. I had to wait for the unit officer's duty shift to start.

The unit officer immediately placed me on barracks restriction after hearing about my actions. I was ordered to stay in the barracks awaiting a disciplinary hearing. I felt at home in the barracks. I knew just about everyone, and there was plenty of work to occupy my time. I fixed chairs, desk drawers, just about anything I would be asked to look at. By the end of the second week other Marines would ask me to fix their pedal bikes and even the neck on a broken guitar. I would use what ever was around to fix anything for anyone. One day I met the Marine who had thrown away the bike that I was riding. He convinced me to sell the bike back to him. I got one hundred dollars for it. The reason I sold the bike was because everyone kept telling me I was going to the brig. Why would I need a bike in the brig, I thought. Plus one hundred dollars I could use when I got out of the brig. The next day I was ordered to report at 0900 hours to the Base Commanders office for my disciplinary hearing.

I ironed my utility uniform so I would look good. I knew this was a disciplinary hearing that I was going to and looking good could help. The idea of why or what this action was about slipped my mind. I reported to the Base commander's office about thirty minutes early and sat down to wait out side the door. The time passed slowly as I watched other Marines working at their jobs. I would let each Marine's life story develop in my mind. This Marine over here has a pitted face he must have come from the mountains where tree branches kept hitting him on the face. Maybe that spit polished Marine over there is a "kiss ass" I became alert when I noticed the Base commander marching down the hall. I jumped to my feet and snapped to attention.

The Major walked past me into his office so I sat back down. I never wore a watch, and there were no clocks in sight, so I did not know how close 0900 hours were. The Officer in charge of the guard (a lieutenant) came down the hall with the Sergeant one step behind him. I snapped to attention as he knocked on the commander's door and entered. The Sergeant ordered that I follow them into the office. One big almost empty room, I thought. A large shiny hardwood desk with a long book case on one wall. Everything on the desk and bookcase was neatly placed. The lieutenant and sergeant sat on a bench for two that was against the other wall from the commander's desk. The Base Commander sitting in the only other chair behind his desk ordered me to stand at attention front and center.

The deep sound of the Major's voice started "This is a serious charge against you PFC Macdonald" He went on to explain the tradition of the Marine Corps and how men like me can destroy it. The way he went on about what I did made me feel guilty. I could have done something that bad? I asked myself. I had no idea what I had done but it must have been outrageous. The Major raised up from his desk to my eye level and his voice echoed a mean attitude as he continued. "Why would a

Marine do something so stupid, and destroy government equipment?" the Major asked. I had no answer. The Major went on as though he did not want that I should reply. "Sergeant" the Major said, "what do you have for a report"? The Major sat back in his desk chair and watched as the Sergeant snapped to attention.

The Sergeant went on to explain a story that was interesting even to me. I did not relate it to me personally because the story was about disobeying orders. I never would disobey an order. The Sergeant explained that I drove a jeep beyond what the Marine Corps calls safe. This story in my mind had nothing to do with me. I tried to be the best Marine I could. I learned from everyone. Everything I did was based on what experienced Marines told me to do. I drove the jeep that way to learn how to handle a jeep that's wheels leave the ground. My mind was darting back and forth trying to relate this day to my life. I lost awareness of what was going on around me. The last words I heard from the Sergeant were, "the charge is flying jeeps in a restricted zone" Those words stuck in my mind. I was jolted back to the talk in the room by the Major's voice. A harsh voice wanted to know how I would answer to this charge.

The Major standing once again face to face looking in my eyes. I knew the voice was his, but I was unaware of what was said. How do I answer? What is the question? The only thing I heard was flying jeeps in a restricted zone. I've never seen a jeep fly. Do they fly? The major moving every muscle on his face demanded in unison with his command, "private you better speak up" I had withdrawn deeper into my mind. I knew jeeps didn't fly. The words came out of my mouth in a sharp commanding voice, "Sir, we all know jeeps don't fly."

The room went silent. The Major sat down in his chair as he dismissed the Sergeant and myself. I heard him order the Lieutenant to stay seated as the door closed behind us. The Sergeant ordered that I continue my barrack restriction as we left the building. I walked back to the barracks, lost at what had happened. The barracks were like a secure zone for me. I got into my normal routine of fixing and cleaning as if that was my job. Two days later I received orders to report to the administration office. The disciplinary decision had been decided. The Commander of El Toro Marine Air Station transferred me off his base. My orders simply told me to report to San Francisco International Airport by a certain time the next day. At that time, I would receive orders to someplace called West Pacific Air Command. I was confused but thought I was on my way to Vietnam.

Chapter Five: Hawaii

San Francisco Airport was where my orders told me to report. I was to receive my ticket at the United Airlines desk. No sooner did I arrived they placed me on a flight with two hundred and thirty-seven other military personnel. Everybody was in their dress uniforms, representing the branch of military service they belong to. I was wearing the perfect Marine Corps dress green uniform that hung in my wall locker for inspection display. I shined the brass and polished my dress shoes every other day. I did this because other Marines warned me of surprise inspections. I never thought about wearing this uniform until the administration officer at El Toro advised me that in order to get on the plane I would need to wear it.

The reaction at the airport was mixed. Some girls and women would look at me starry-eyed. One girl blew me a kiss. I didn't understand why this uniform attracted girls. I just wanted to get out of it, because it was uncomfortable. The men mostly ignored me as I walked past. I did notice the words "war monger" or "baby killer" muttered as I passed some people. I assumed a lot of people were talking about the same subject, so I just continued on my path. The closer I got to the military terminal the more concentrated the numbers of military personnel became.

At the terminal, I learned I would fly a DC-10 from San Francisco to Honolulu non-stop. The flight would be approximately seven hours long, with two meals served. I was told to report to a Marine Sergeant at the terminal desk in Honolulu. I would receive my final orders to the Far East at that time. I was the last passenger to get on the plane before the doors closed. There was only one empty seat, which meant I would be located next to the aisle. I remember taxiing down the runway then the next thing I knew we were on final approach and my ears hurt from the pressure changes.

The beauty of the island overwhelmed everyone as we got off the plane. Women in grass skirts greeted us with a flower as we entered the terminal. The airport was filled with the sound of Hawaiian music to relax your mind. Everybody was smiling and giving a friendly (aloha) to one another. The paradise of Hawaii was on display right in the airport. Water fountains were scattered along the corridors. Kukui trees circled the fountains filled with colorful flowers crowding the circle around the trees. Bright pink, red, and yellow orchids engulf your eyes as you walk down the trail through the terminal. I thought I was dreaming: everything was so neat and clean it didn't seem real.

The Marine Sergeant at the desk brought me back to real life. He called out my name and rank "Lance Corporal Macdonald" as I passed his desk. ""Yes, Sergeant" I replied " this where I pick up my orders?" The Sergeant ordered that I hang around his desk area until he could get me a flight number. The time was approaching 0900 hours when I first sat on the bench across from the Sergeant's desk. The crowd of people kept increasing as the day progressed. People were beginning to fill every square inch of the airport terminal. I kept admiring how the Hawaiian people continued to be friendly and help other people. I was still in uniform, which in a strange way gave people a sense of trust in me. I would see a lady pulling to many pieces of luggage so I would assist her. People would be confused so I would guide them to the information desk. Mothers with children would need to sit and take a break. I would play with their children to pass the time while they took that needed break.

The time was 1300 hours when I looked at the clock above the Sergeant's head. He smiled implying to me that I needed to wait longer so I said nothing. That is when a large airport transit rack of luggage being pushed by this little guy tipped over. The little person was struggling to tip the cart up right. I instinctively started helping upright the cart and replace the luggage on it. The airport worker was dressed in a loose airport uniform with short dark hair. We worked side by side loading the items as a team, which only took a few minutes. After we finished loading the worker turned to thank me, that is when I realized it was a woman. We talked for a few minutes then she was gone.

I continued to wait for my flight number as the afternoon pasted. I met a lot of people, talking and helping with who or whatever. The luggage girl I had helped earlier noticed me as she was walking past my area. She stopped and asked, "Why are you still here?" I told her I was ordered to wait here. In a shocked voice she informed me it was past six PM and everyone is gone for the weekend. She then explained how the Sergeant must have forgotten me. This lady introduced her self as Morta as she picked up a nearby phone. The phone conversation seemed intense for a few minutes as Morta's facial expression described her serious mood. The news of what she found out over the phone shocked me. She told me the next military flight was 1100 o'clock Monday morning. I thought to myself, that is three days away. Morta sensed the confusion of my body language from the news that she just had given me.

Morta sat down beside me on the bench in a way that gave me a sense of security. We talked about where I was going and how exciting being in the Marine Corps was. The words came so easy in talking to Morta. I relaxed as if Morta had been my friend forever. The conversation switched from me to her life after a while. I learned that she was thirty-nine years old and lived alone. Her husband was a surf king on the island until he died in a surfing accident almost one year ago.

Morta asked me about my family. I explained how I didn't really know them, although I do write a letter once a week to a person called my mother. Morta's interest grew as I explained about the accident. She questioned about my being a Marine and other things concerning my mental ability. The time had now gone past the late evening hours. Morta asked if I wanted to spend the weekend with her camping. I was reluctant because of the Sergeant's orders to remain in the area of his desk. Morta explained again about the next military flight in a way that persuaded me she was correct. This was great but I explained how my duffel bag and other stuff were at the airport so I couldn't leave. This lady, reassuring my childish reluctance, established in my mind that airport transit would hold it for my next flight. The conversation switched to talk about changing my clothes and that I need items to brush my teeth and wash myself with? Morta gave me some clothes that airport workers use to do maintenance dressed in. Questions I had about the clothes were answered when Morta told me to get the things I needed. She assured me with her next sentence, that no one would see me because we were going camping. I was to bring only the basic items. I took the shirt and shorts into the head and changed my clothes. Morta took my uniform when I came out and placed them on a hanger in her wall locker with my handbag that once contained my toothbrush. I left the locker room carrying just my toothbrush and the manila envelope containing my military records.

Morta was leading me out of the building heading to the parking lot. What a place I thought to myself. I enjoyed the beauty of the building so much I almost didn't want to go out side. The sun was gone but the darkness of night was still away off; I noticed as we entered the exit doorway. Once out side the surrounding scenery was prettier than inside. The temperature was about seventy-seven degrees with a soft ocean breeze. The palm trees lightly blowing in a fanning motion, as if waving to the people. Flowers in full bloom of many different colors being momentary shaded by the moving palm leaves. This moving shade caused the color of the flowers to change like they were signaling everyone to relax and enjoy life. The streets and sidewalks were as clean as the floor inside the terminal. I followed Morta across the street and into the almost empty parking lot.

Morta walked up to a 350cc Honda motor cycle and hooked her backpack on the back of the sissy bar. The bike was red with two purple helmets hooked under the seat so they hung off to one side. The seat was two levels, the driver sat about six inches lower than the passenger. The Hawaiian theme of a colorful design made the seat stand out from the rest of the bike. Two large saddlebags hung one on each side of the bike. All I could think was, how is this small old woman gonna even move the machine? Morta was lucky if she was even five feet tall. Her weight might be one hundred pounds if that. The tips of her toes stretched hard to reach the ground in order for her to pushed the bike of the kickstand. The bike engine started as Morta said,

"OK get on." I carefully climbed in back of Morta hoping she could hold us long enough to get started in forward motion. My feet were firmly resting on the pegs above the mufflers as I sat back against the sissy bar. The bike started to move as I grabbed for Morta's waist but I was to high and my hands went over her chest. I quickly pulled my hands back and held onto her shoulders. Morta leaned back and told me to relax and enjoy the ride. This girl could handle a motorcycle quite well, I thought as we sped down the street.

The paradise just kept getting better as we traveled down route 78. I thought I saw a sign identifying the highway but with so much going on I didn't really care. The scenery of the city seemed as clean and colorful all the way to where the houses disappeared and the forests began. The people, buildings, and cars were getting less and less in number. The highway became a dirt road but I am not sure at what point this happen. My head was twisting and turning in an attempt to see everything. We were now going up small hills as the trees and bushes crowded the edge of the road. Soon the dirt road turned into a path just wide enough for the bike to travel through. Morta stopped the bike deep into the woods at the edge of a small waterfall. Paradise just turned to heaven, I thought as we got off the bike.

Morta seemed relaxed and at home as she moved around doing things. She took a small tent from one of the saddlebags and we assembled it together. I don't think she needed my help but she smiled as I tried to put the poles together. A few feet away there was what appeared to be an old campfire. Morta walked past that area to some bushes. She reached in and opened up a storage trunk full of camping gear. Handing me a flashlight she suggested we go get some firewood before it got too late. Into the dark of the woods we went. This woman scuffled back and forth picking up dead branches and other parts of trees until we both had an arm full of firewood. Heading back to the campsite Morta reached out and held my hand that had the flashlight in it. I thought of the airport where the mothers led their children to control them.

We didn't go that far into the woods, so Morta holding my hand didn't last long. We were back in the campsite in a few seconds. Morta demonstrated how to start a campfire in a friendly helpful way. She did it in a way to make it look like a natural teaching process so I would learn. I was now sitting facing the waterfall that splashed into a pool of water at its bottom. The stars that reflected in the water moved by the ripples created by the waterfall hitting the water. The campfire sat between the water and me as the flicker of the flames started to appear in the water. The fire seemed to add a new life to the one being played so patiently by the action in the water. Morta got a bottle of whiskey out of her saddlebag and sat on the opposite side of the campfire. The waterfall gave the allusion of falling down the back of her head. This along with the ripples that appeared as if the water was coming out from under made the picture look magical. The sounds of the birds singing in the woods around us gave me a warm tingle inside.

Morta started talking to me about my car accident as she looked up and asked, "Would you want some whiskey?" I said "yes" then went on to explained how I did not remember anything in my life that happened before I woke up at Portsmouth Naval Hospital. The questions were friendly and coming from her in a soft voice. I just answered them openly as if we were talking about someone else. I am sure that there was some degree of disbelief on her part as whether to believe me or not. I had no understanding of what disbelief was so it didn't faze me that people thought I was exaggerating or lying. I had no concept of time or memory of my life before the accident. The conversation soon moved to talking about my time at Marine Air Base El Toro California. I could remember bits and pieces of things that happened while I was there but I was vague as to exactly what might have happen. I just started talking about my experiences there as I relaxed by the fire. The amazing thing was when I would be telling one thing something else that happened would pop into my head. I would, without any fore thought, add that on to the story. I had the sequences of events wrong in telling the story but I could not remember which order the events happen to me. I was starting to have a past life to talk about. The feeling of starting to remember things to talk about filled my head with joy.

The subject we were talking about changed when Morta asked, "Is the trouble you got in why you left El Toro?" I started telling her about my wish to be a good Marine. I explained that to do so I needed to go to Vietnam. I identified war as a Marine's primary job. She did not feel anyone should go to war to fight because politicians want to look good. The thought of the retired Sergeant at Portsmouth Naval Hospital came into my thoughts as Morta stopped talking. I started telling Morta about him what I could recall. How he was a great Marine who could do anything. We talked back and forth about my past and what I believed my future would be. The night slipped away into the early morning hours. The whiskey and the relaxing conversation put us both to sleep right where we sat.

The next morning at 0500 hours the birds were singing and the sun shining my eyes slowly opened. I just sat in my spot enjoying the area in the daylight. I could now see the water poured off a rock that stuck out of the ledge about thirty feet up a steep hill. Bushes, vines and flowers covered the ledge on both sides of the waterfall all the way to the top. Below the waterfall was a large pool of water that was crystal clear. The splash from the water falling landed about ten feet from the back edge of the pool. Surrounding the edge was bushes out to the edge of the forest. A rock by the campfire extended out into the pool about five feet just under the top edge of the water. This appeared to be the only way in. Morta was still sleeping so I quietly stood up and walked to the pool entrance.

I reached down and touched the water causing little ripples that were over whelmed by the larger ones created by the fall. I checked Morta to see if she was still sleeping then started to take my clothes off. I quietly walked out on the entrance rock not wanting to wake Morta up. A loud "Whoops!" and a big loud splash as I hit the water. The rock stopped and the depth of the water went straight down. I swam back to the rock and looked to check on if I had woken Morta. Morta had rolled over but appeared to be still sleeping peacefully. I got my clothes and was rubbing them together under the waterfall as if washing them. I figured that at least I could get the dirt out. I let the waterfall on my head as I rubbed my body trying to get the dirt off me also. I then thought this is crazy. I have no clothes to wear until these are dry. It didn't matter. Morta surprised me when she came up from behind me under the water. She was naked also. I could see her butt as she swam past me to some bushes hanging over the edge of the pool. She soon swam back with a hand full of leaves. First handing some leaves to me she picked up my shirt and demonstrated how to wash my cloths with them. The leaves made my clothes smell fresh and clean. After we finished washing all my clothes Morta through them over some bushes near the entrance to the pool so they would dry.

The next few hours we just swam and talked. The day was perfect with the temperature about 82 degrees. There was a light wind and not a cloud in the sky. I was nervous at first swimming with an old woman with no clothes on. Morta was so easy to talk with, her words removing any fear I may have had. Morta must have felt the nervousness at the start. We talked about friendship and what it meant to her. Soon we were playing tag or racing across the pool. My nervousness turned to a trust that bonded us. I felt Morta and I had been a friend forever. I felt like I belonged here with her but I had many questions such as why she came here alone on weekends. She explained how this was where her husband liked to come. This place reminded her of him. The washing clothes with the leaves and swimming before fully waking up were special things they did together. I was the first person she has ever brought to this place although at certain times of the year quite a few people come here for fun. Morta explained how if other people were here she would take a quick swim, then hike into the mountains. This was her place and time to be with her late husband, whom she missed so much.

The conversation went back and forth between us. I was trying to learn everything I could about what ever. Morta knew what berries to eat and what berries not to eat. We picked a variety of different types of samples to try. Some were tart, other were sweet like Morta was becoming to me. Some berries Morta told me were poisonous as she showed me how to identify which berries not to eat. Her vast knowledge became apparent as she went on. She explained that a person needs to always know direction, whereever you are. This is always handy she said. This lead into talking about the direction of the sun and stars in the sky. How at night, cloudy days or just when you are deep into the woods you can not always see the sun. Morta showed me how to look at trees and rocks to find which way north was. We were keeping so busy that when I got hot, without even thinking I took my shirt off. Morta reached out at that moment to a tree and picked a nut-like fruit off it. She slammed it against the trunk of the tree until it cracked. The open shell had creamy oil that Morta rubbed on my upper body. "There" she said, "this will stop the sun from burning you".

The conversation fascinated Morta, because I got along so well but had no memory. She kept probing with questions as if to catch a sign that I was faking my memory loss. The questions such as, did I loose my money gambling? My answers were always honest if I could remember what she was talking about. I answered the gambling question, explaining that I only got paid twenty-one dollars a month so I could not spend money on something I did not need. This answer brought on questions why I got so little pay. I went on to explain how my father told me ninety percent of my paycheck was to be allotted to him in New Hampshire. The subject ended with my saying, "I never have had any extra money so I guess I don't miss it." Morta stopped me and said let's go for a hike.

Morta got a small knapsack and put a bottle of whiskey and a few other things in it. She waved her arm and said, "follow me" and off into the woods we went. I stopped Morta every once in a while and ask her a question or two. I learned about trees grown on the island. There was the Kukui, which I had heard earlier was the Hawaiian State tree. Morta pointed several out as they grew naturally in the forest. She explained how it's also called the candlenut tree, because it produces oil used to make candles and dyes. She told me a story of how she and her husband tried making some when they started their own business. They read books on the early settlers of the island producing the candles to sell to the tourists. They started the business but never succeeded in the venture. Every time she mentioned her late husband a soft smile and a comfortable look would appear on Morta's face.

Morta walked over to the side of the path we were walking on. She placed her hand on a tree and called it a Monkeypod tree. I smiled and asked her if I should believe that name. That lead to a story of the island industry of bowls and dishes and how it related to her family. Her relations along time ago would make bowls and dishes by hand from the Monkeypod trees. They sold these items to rich tourist as their only means to make money. Now her parents ran the factory that produces what her grandparents made by hand many years earlier.

The tree I liked the best was the autograph tree. Morta started writing on a leaf from this type tree. I assumed she was teasing me. After a few minutes she signaled me to stand beside her. The leave still hanging from a branch had writing on it from Morta. "Peter, you're a great friend." She told me the words would grow with the tree and our friend ship would grow with it. I asked if it would be ok if I wrote something to her. She handed me a stick and I wrote, "You're my dear sweet friend forever." Morta leaned over to me and put her lips to my cheek and kissed it. I turned bright red.

The breadfruit tree was the tastiest though. We were walking through the woods playing tag and hide and seek as Morta stopped by this tree and sat down. She asked me to shake the tree just for a minute. The request sounded funny but I did it anyhow. Ten pieces of fruit fell to the ground all around her. She picked two pieces up and handed one to me. She took a bit of the piece still in her hand. I then took a bit to find out it tasted like bread. We lay under the tree and talked while we ate and rested. The talk continued between us building a bond that would last forever. We could say anything and trust the other not to laugh or take it wrong.

We hiked for several more hours until the sun started to set. I asked Morta how far the campsite was? She waved her arms with the words "right here" as she started to gather rocks to start a campfire. I collected the firewood and started the fire. We sat down on opposite sides of the fire and started passing the bottle of whiskey back and forth. We talked as we had the night before until the wee hours of the morning. We both fell asleep in the same positions by the campfire.

The next morning I woke up first. I started collecting berries like Morta had taught me. A wide assortment of berries filled the basket I had made with my tee shirt. Hours passed as I circled the campsite while Morta slept. I kept peeking at her until she started to move. I knew she would wake up soon. I placed the manila folder with my records in it on the ground next to her to act as a plate. Acting as a servant, I poured the berries onto the plate for breakfast in bed at nature's hotel. Morta woke shortly after I sat down next to the plate and smiled at me. We started talking as if we never ran out of things to say. Eating and talking as the berries soon dwindled down to the last one on the plate. I was eating the last berry as Morta asked; "Don't you wonder what's in there?" I explained once again how the Corporal sealed the envelope and ordered me not to break the seal. She took the envelope and put some whiskey on the seal. The envelope opened as if it was never sealed. An expression of satisfaction emerged from this innocent looking woman in a devious way. Morta slowly opened the file explaining how the mystery of my Marine life was about to be exposed. In a slow steady voice she stated that I was stationed at El Toro. Then a few minutes later she went on to express how the record doesn't mention my armory or guard duty tours. She went on to claim how it does not even mention my trouble that I got into. I just said, "Who knows? Maybe they don't put stuff like that in there." Morta rationalized "maybe I was there such a short time the paper work is still on some ones desk and never got filed." We talked for a while longer about different subjects. The morning was coming to an end and we needed to start back to the pool. We cleaned up the area and headed back to the waterfall.

The hike was just as interesting as the day before. Every so often we would stop and sit on a rock or stump. The sounds around us were enchanting. The birds were filling the air with songs of love to each other. The animals running and dancing while they looked for food and played with each other. They all seemed to ignore us as we sat side by side enjoying the friendship that was growing.

Just then a bird walked within inches of us. Morta's hand in a quick flash grabbed the bird by the neck. She claimed in a soft voice so not to disturb the other animals "this is lunch". Then she snapped the bird's neck as she stated, "Survival is eating what you can catch." Morta held the bird by its feet in one hand and held my hand with her other. She slowly started walking through the woods as we continued our hike.

We got back to the pool where the motor cycle was parked by late afternoon. I started a campfire while watching Morta clean and gut the bird. "You learned quickly" Morta commented, because the fire started so effortlessly. She then took a metal rod off the back of her bike and speared it through the bird. I asked, "If that is what the rod is for?" Morta explained how her late husband had shown her to look around and use whatever will work. She went on to tell me her husband favorite saying was "Surviving is making the best with what you have." Slowly placing the speared bird over the fire, Morta stood up and walked toward the pool entrance. She started removing her clothes as she said, "Come on, let's wash our clothes". We swam for hours. Every so often, Morta would climb out of the pool to rotate the bird. I would turn red as her naked body cleared the surface of the water. Trying to hide my eyes, which were attracted toward her, I would sink in the pool, sneaking a prolonged peek as her back was toward me.

My clothes were still wet hanging on the bushes because the sun had gone down. I was reluctant when Morta gave one of her shirts and shorts to me to put on. I looked at her as if to say (Marines Don't wear women's clothes) but Morta responded to my look "you use what you have to survive". I put on the clothes as I took a seat across from Morta at the campfire. She picked up a tree branch about one half-inch thick and broke two six-inch pieces off it. I was amazed as she jammed each piece on opposite ends of the metal rod holding the bird. She then picked up the bird and took a bite. We passed the bird back and forth between us. I was excited as I stated to Morta "What a great meal--berries and bird by an open fire." We talked into the night as the evening slipped away and we fell asleep on opposite sides of the campfire.

The next morning Morta woke up before the sun came above the horizon. I was still in Morta's clothes as she placed a leaf on my chest and told me to "get up". I watched her as she broke the leave so oil came out. Sticking her finger under the broken leave, the oil dripped on the top of it. Quickly she started brushing her teeth with the finger. I tried brushing my teeth and was pleased to taste of a clean fresh feeling in my mouth. We jumped in the pool for a quick swim to wash our bodies one more time. After that we picked up the campsite and put everything in its place before we were ready to go.

Morta, looking at me with a sweet expression on her face asked if, "I want to drive back to the airport." I told her "Yes" but I explained how I had no idea how. Morta demonstrated how to shift and brake on a bike. After the lesson I was eager to try as we started down the path. I had a big smile on my face reflecting Morta's trust in me to drive her bike. Once we were back on the dirt road Morta leaned back against the sissy bar as a sign of trust. I felt her hand releasing my chest only to be replaced by her legs wrapping around me. We cruised down the road as Morta talked and gave me directions how to get back to the airport. The time was seven-thirty as we entered the airport parking lot on another bright sunny day.

Morta quickly took me back to the locker room so I could get my uniform on. We each finished changing at the same time so Morta walked me back to the terminal desk. The Sergeant wasn't there yet so the two of us sat on a bench next to each other and held hands. The area was busy but not crowded as the other day. Morta holding both my hands with hers talked about how she "Loved every minute of the past two days." She told me how comfortable it made her feel that I never made a pass at her. After a few seconds pause her eyes turned sad as she asked me if there was a reason why I had not. I just looked at her and said, "Why would I?" She seemed dumbfounded and said "I guess you really are a child up there, (pointing toward my head) with a man's body." Morta stood up put her lips to mine giving me a long sensuous kiss, which I reciprocated. In a soft voice near my ear as she hugged me tight said, "I have to check in for work. Wait here for me." Morta released me and hurried across the room taking a quick look over her shoulder at me until she disappeared.

The Marine Sergeant spoke to me in a stern voice not five minutes after Morta left. "Where the hell have you been? Your plane leaves in two minutes. Hurry!" The Sergeant grabbed my orders as we passed his desk. Ordering me to move faster as we traveled down the ramp to a closing plane door. He handed me my orders as the door closed between us. I sat down quickly to lookout the window. I could see the desk, but I did not see Morta. I was on my way again to my next stop.

Chapter Six: West P.A.C

The plane was filled with over two hundred military personnel on there way west. I was on a military transport in route to my next duty station. For the first two hours of the flight I slept soundly, only to be awakened by the person in the window seat who needed to go the head. This disruption caused the person seated on the other side of me to say "Hi" and we began talking to each other. I learned his name was Joe and that Texas was his home state. Joe called himself a cowboy even though he lived in the city of Dallas. His description of what Texas was like sounded pretty close to life around El Toro, where I just came from. Crowds of people rushing to get places. Tall buildings with large corporations and streets filled with cars. I asked him about riding horses and roping cows like I watched on the TV program, Rawhide. Joe told me he never had seen a cow or rode a horse, but girls love Texas cowboys. He told me that being from Texas makes him a cowboy. I accepted that as some kind of rule. I believed he was a cowboy.

The Navy dude came back from the head in just a few minutes. He introduced himself to Joe and me with his name, Fred. Chicago was Fred's hometown. City life was the only way to live according to Fred. Everything you could ever need was within walking distance. He described his favorite restaurant, which was a sub shop around the corner from his apartment. They served a great sausage onion and mushroom sub that required a beer while eating it. He seemed to be hung up on the number of girls available living in his neighborhood that would date him. The next few hours were spent learning about things Joe and Fred had done. The one fact both men agreed on is non-military flights are better because the stewardesses are prettier.

The conversation continued hours into the flight when Joe made the statement "What about you Pete"? I just looked up and said, "I don't know much about me." It never dawned on me no one would understand a statement like that. Joe and Fred were intrigued that anyone could make such a statement, never mind it being true. They kept needling me that I must work for the (C.I.A), or maybe I was a spy. I did not realize the miscommunication that was taking place. Everyone within hearing range was interested in my story about complete loss of memory. I became an item for the disbelieves to mock. They used sarcasm to get their negative point across. The believers tried to pump me (as if I was a suspect in a police interrogation) for information to support their theory. The conversation turned to a question and answer game. I did not realize the miscommunication had evolved to an interrogation session. The probing questions of Joe and Fred turned into a drama for the flight's entertainment. From my point of view, I had trouble comprehending why these men didn't understand there was nothing in my head about when I grew up. Alton was a lost memory.

Joe asked me the basic questions in the beginning like "What state are you from?" I answered all the questions as honestly as I could, but the uncertainty of my answers was picked up by others. I said, "New Hampshire I guess?" Then Fred or someone else would respond, "New Hampshire--what do you mean you guess?" The statement (don't you know what state you're from), would be an attempt to put me on the defensive. I, being naïve, responded in an open honest manner as if the conversation was just friendly talk. The conversation continued like this for some time. Joe and Fred digging in and attempting to prove I was just pulling their leg. The tensions grew as I tried to explain if there is nothing to remember you just don't know. This casual attitude of honest relaxed answers changed the motives of the questioners. The men were on a mission to prove that I was faking my memory loss.

Fred came out with the statement type question that seemed to show I was lying. "If you have no memory how come you are in the military and your pay grade is (E-3). His question had two purposes that went right past me. The first reason was to make me mad. The questioners thought this would make me slip up and tell the truth. The second reason was to corner my truthful ness with facts that I couldn't justify. A person who is mad and cornered will naturally tell different stories and give the others something to being out the truth with. I bit on neither one of their attempts to catch me with a lie or misstatement. The fact was I had no memory, so I was already telling the truth. I couldn't slip up if I had no knowledge of what Fred and Joe were attempting to do.

The flight had been ten hours long to this point. The others, still not believing my memory loss, were growing tired of their failure to prove I was a fake. The pilot interrupted everyone to make the announcement at this point. We were on final approach to some place called Midway Island. Everyone turned their head to the nearest window as the pilot said to buckle your seat belts. The windows were black; night had fallen. Everyone leaned back in their seats and followed the pilot's orders at the same time. The whole process was like a planned maneuver as everyone moved in sequence. Feeling the pain in my ears from the drop in the plane's altitude, I started chewing some gum. I kept thinking about the others comments and the way they could hardly believe my memory was gone. This negative feeling built inside my head. The questions that the mind of a ten-year-old asks are inquisitive. My undeveloped mind could not answer these questions which led to my being confused. I was at the beginning of realizing I was different than the other people around me.

Joe and Fred, not wanting to admit my amnesia was real, kept asking me questions. We left the plane together and walked across the taxiway into the passenger building. We said good-bye to each other as our destinations took us to separate areas of the building. Joe and Fred would be getting back on the same plane after it is refueled. I would get on another plane headed for Tokyo, Japan in one hour.

I didn't know what to do. I was sitting in a metal building alone in the middle of nowhere next to a runway. The darkness of night made it unlikely I would learn anything outside so I just sat there looking around. A one-hour hold over stretched to over two hours before I boarded a different type plane. This plane had a large gray body. On the outside of the tail were the markings C-141 stenciled in large black paint. Inside the plane gave the appearance of a large warehouse filled with metal containers. We were directed to a section of the plane for personal to ride. No stewardess or movies made this a long, boring flight. I took out my personnel event logbook to write some notes in before I forgot the events that were happening.

Along with the correspondence course I started to take at El Toro, I also took a letter writing course. The Marine Corps, for public relations reasons, had ordered each base to promote letter writing. The course was free and it supported the idea of the English course I was taking at the time. The course was one hour once a week held in our barracks recreation room. I only attended two classes because I left El Toro so quickly, but I picked up ideas on how to write letters. The trick that stuck in my mind was to write notes in a log or journal book of things that happen. If you do this within a reasonable time after something happens the facts are clear. This way you remember the little details to look at when you write a letter later on in time. I found if I had the time I would (after I finished the log) try to write one paragraph a day of a letter to someone. I was now writing letters to this woman called my mother and a girl that lived in a small town near Alton. I had no memory of either person, but responded as if I remembered because they were my connection to my civilian past.

Once we were airborne a cockpit person stuck his head into the area and said the seat belt light is off. Some of the men got up to move around and stretched. On the other planes I had flown on, everyone had to stay seated with their seat belt on. This time there were only about twenty men as passengers. Some I had seen on the other plane from Hawaii. One man, who was sitting behind me on the other plane I remembered because he interrupted the conversation several times. After about an hour into the flight he walked over to where I was sitting. The conversation that started was about the trip so far and each of our experiences. The questions seemed like a repeat from the last flight. It seemed to me like everyone asks the same questions to start a conversation with someone new: Where are you coming from? Did you stop any place?

I talked about my time at El Toro. My memory of the events that took place at El Toro was short bits and pieces. I knew I was on guard duty at the ammo bunkers during my stay there. I knew I was on the 1700 hours to 0600-hour shift. The more specific facts like names of streets or bunker identification numbers were a blank to me. One of the other Marines on the flight was a grunt. That is a ground pounder, also called a foot soldier. He was holding an M-16 rifle slung over his shoulder with the barrel pointed down. The grunt asked me about different items pertaining to the roving patrol at El Toro. I answered some questions but others I had no memory of. It turns out the grunt just left guard duty at El Toro and he was testing me. I must have failed the test because the disbeliveers among the other men became apparent. I qualified my lack of knowledge with the statement that I wasn't on guard duty that long. The others accepted that and started questioning me on what else I did at El Toro.

I told the men I was a (MAG) armor. My job was to clean, repair, and inventory over three thousand weapons. This immediately caused someone to make the statement about the amount of time that it would take to do a job like that. I explained I was only at the armory a couple months total but I worked long hours. The questions of disbelief started again. After awhile the questions got down to the individual names of the parts to an M-16 rifle. I couldn't even remember the name of a firing pin. The disbelieves were having a field day discrediting the events I would talk about. I took no offense because I was naive to what was happening.

Finally the grunt did the ultimate test. He handed me his M-16 and said, "If you were an armor take this apart." In a matter of seconds his weapon was stripped down to its stock. Everyone was quiet in deep amazement at the speed and accuracy of my actions. I told him his weapon was a disgrace because it had dirt on some of the parts. I took the grunt's cleaning kit and cleaned and polished every part as I reassembled the M-16 rifle. I noticed the firing pin had a crack in it. I advised the grunt to report the damaged firing pin at his next base because it needed to be replaced. The disbeliveers were now confused. Does he have amnesia or not?

One Marine wanted to ask a question or just identify with my life. Finally he couldn't hold back any more as he moved closer to me with his hand out. He said skeptically, "I heard you telling guys in the last flight you didn't remember you're past life." I looked at Bill with his hand out to shake, while telling me his name. I again stated, "My life that I know started about a year or two ago." I continued telling the story about how I woke up at Portsmouth Naval Hospital one day. The other Marines around us were listening intensely as I spoke about how I met some people called my parents. I stated that I think I have brothers and sisters from letters I receive from my mother. I qualified that with the works "but I'm not sure." I had little memory about the hospital but I did remember the retired Marine. Bill gasped with a smile before I could say another word. He blurted out "I wish I could forget my past." I just looked at him with a questioning expression on my face. I tried to explain, "If you don't remember, you can't be happy because you don't know you're happy ".

The pilot was now announcing our approach to Tokyo International Airport in Japan.

He told us to "Sit down and fasten our seat belts." I started chewing gum to help reduce the pain in my ears, like I was accustom to doing. The landing didn't seem any different than any other landing had before. Inside the airport was different than the other airports I recalled. The only people speaking English were the military personnel. The other people spoke a foreign language. I had no idea what they were saying to each other. The clothes they wore were different too, mostly bright and colorful robes. I followed a few people around trying to make out what they were saying to each other. I didn't get far in that effort because within minutes a Marine grabbed me for my next flight. I was now on a C-117 headed for Marine Air Base, Futema, Okinawa.

A C-117 is a small two-engine propeller driven aircraft. This style plane dated back to World War II as a cargo and troop transport. The noise in the plane was like sitting in a metal box with someone beating the sides. The only means of communication was to yell at each other. This trip seemed to take forever because of the idle time just sitting trying to ignore the noise. The actual time we were in the air was only four hours, but our ears were ringing for many hours afterwards.

Futema seemed strictly military. The only things you saw were American military personnel and vehicles. I just kept searching the area around me in amazement as I got into the jeep that came to pick me up. We drove on a clean black tarred road with mowed lawns on each side. This road led us around the end of the runway. On the other side of the road from the runway were rows of metal containers. The numbers seemed in the thousands of row after row after row. I asked the driver, "What is in the rows of metal boxes?" The driver explained

"Futema is a Marine Air Base Wing supply and repair station." He pointed to the acres of containers and stated "Over there each row is a complete air base unit ready for deployment." He pointed over to the other side and said "Over there is a repair squadron where they fix broken air base units." Once on the other side of the runway, we saw the barracks off to one side. They were four story concrete buildings like at El Toro Marine Air Base California. I was lost in excitement and a bit of fear at the same time. What was happening at the present in my life? Any memory or thoughts of the past were a blank in my mind. Where am I? What will become of me? Can I relate to the other Marines here? My mind was spinning questions so fast they could not be answered. I took my duffel bag out of the jeep and headed into the barracks to my new home.

The memory of the flight from Hawaii kept flashing in my thoughts. I had many questions such as, am I different than other Marines? The phrase loss of memory and the word amnesia kept repeating over and over in my mind. I now was aware, but still too young in my mind to comprehend the meaning and consequences of my medical condition.

Chapter Seven: The Lesson

My new home was an island sixty miles long and five miles wide called Okinawa. I was to live in a two-man room on the second floor of a four story concrete building. I was in a strange land trying to grasp a sense of reality, what ever it might be. This is where I met Steve, a Private First Class, who was my roommate. His home state was Florida, where his parents still lived. This was Steve's sixth month of his tour. This meant he had reached the halfway point to go back to the states unless he extended his tour. His job in Okinawa was working in the administration office of the MABS unit that I was to be stationed with. The time seemed to pass really quickly that first night of my stay in Okinawa. Steve talked to me while I unpacked my duffel bag and arranged my wall locker. The change in time, crossing so many times zones in my travel, made me fall asleep early in the evening. No sooner had I put my head on the pillow than the time to wake up had arrived. This was my first full day in a new country. What would it be like?

Steve seemed to be a nice person. He wanted to show me the ropes of checking into the base. First it was breakfast at the typical Marine Corps mess hall. This was going to be my home for the next year, I thought to myself as we left the mess hall for the base administration office. I told Steve before checking into this base; I needed to fill out transfer forms. Steve didn't understand and questioned about the logic of doing that. I explained a little but soon forgot what I was talking about, my interests absorbed in the many events happening around me. Planes taking off and landing, men in uniform moving at a quick pace back and forth, my questions were too many to worry about answering Steve. The policy to check in on this base was that I had to just to drop my travel orders off at the main office. While at the base administration office I was told which MABS unit I was assigned to. Steve knew where I was going but we had to go through the process anyhow.

Steve flagged down a duce and a half (a large military truck). He recognized the person who was driving. The Marine agreed to give us a ride to our MABS unit on the other side of the runway. The building we entered looked like a garage or gas station, the typical filling station seen in every city state side. A diesel pump located in a large tarred area in front of the garage. People working on engines and machinery in and out of the building. We walked through the work area to a door that entered the office for the administration section of the unit. Just inside the door was the unit-commanding officer, filling a cup at the coffee machine. Steve introduced us to each other.

The word of my request for a transfer must have traveled by airmail. The Commanding officer acknowledged my presence in the typical Marine Corps dominating manner. The cold eyes, motionless face, and strong deep voice started to explain the unit's expectation of every Marine who is a part of his unit. He went on to explain everyone does their job without error, follow orders and never breaks the chain of command. The question or command for an answer followed next. Why did I put in for a transfer? I told the Commanding Officer in a respectful deep voice, "That is what a good Marine does, who wants to go to Vietnam."

I was assigned to stripping, rebuilding, and painting absorbers. I had no idea what an absorber was. I would soon learn that my M.O.S. 7011 (Launch and Recovery) was shooting planes off a runway, like they do on an aircraft carrier. The absorber was the break for stopping planes with a hook when it returns to the base. My mind flashed back to my first days at El Toro. The absorber was what I started to work on before being sent to learn guard duty. Then when I was on guard duty I watched a plane use the tail hook while landing. A plane doing six to seven hundred knots drops a tail hook from under the rear wings and catches a wire rope that is stretched across the runway. I was fascinated at the time by the enormous, fast action of every thing around me. The connection between what I was witnessing at this time in Okinawa and the absorber at El Toro did not register in my mind. The word absorber made me think of El Toro but the connection did not register. I was unknowingly building a catalog of information in my mind as most people do from childhood.

I started working in the MABS garage that first day. I worked hard and asked questions about every part of the absorber. I seemed to have a need to understand what each part did. The individual names of each piece I would forget the second after being told. However the function, no matter how technical, I would remember. I learned how the wire rope is hooked to the nylon strap, which is spun around a reel. The reel sits on top of the main body of the absorber. The absorber is made up of channels for water to flow. The center or movable part, which is attached to the reel, channels the water in one direction. The stationary body (or reservoir) channels the water in the opposite direction. This creates what is called a vortex action. The faster the reel is pulled the stronger the breaking action resists the pull on the wire rope. My questions were building friendships and introducing me to working as a team member. I found it was easier to talk as I was asking questions if I was helping that person with something while we were working. The men appreciated my helping without being asked. I was helping others while I learned. I did not realize the bond that was building with everyone I had contact with.

Rebuilding absorbers was a new experience that excited me. My first week was structural in learning to take an absorber apart. Each absorber we worked on was dismantled down to individual pieces. Separately each piece would be striped down to bare metal as if it were new. These pieces were cleaned, and at that time they were checked for damage. If the part was in usable condition it got painted and signed off a log sheet by who ever worked on it. I kept busy learning how to calibrate the tolerances of different parts of the assembly. Setting break pucks seemed simple but were a process of it's own. There was a special technique to the break puck assembly. The more I did the more I wanted to know. My mind kept absorbing information, even though my short-term memory could not remember when asked.

The fascination of each part of the absorber intrigued me. I would test ways of reusing parts as a way to learn more about them. The used parts after I cleaned and repaired them would be as good as any new parts. I saw no need to replace parts even through our supply room had every part ten times over what was needed. I thought, why waste these parts if I could clean and reuse it. Plus I was advised not to reuse parts, which made me want to try getting away with it.

Part of rebuilding is to be able to locate and retrieve parts and equipment needed. The supply room was a room filled with millions of small packages containing single parts. Each part had a serial number identifying it. The serial number located the parts in the supply area. The supply yard was a staging area for complete air bases and large individual parts. Code numbers stenciled on the outside of the metal containers identified these parts. The graveyard was at the end of the staging area. This was where parts in poor shape are stored until salvage orders allow them to be removed. I was only a Lance Corporal (e-3) and had to take orders from anyone senior to me (almost every one was my boss). This meant I was a "gofer". A person to retrieve parts that were needed. I enjoyed the mystery of locating parts. Everything was in perfect order on every shelf in the supply room. Our MABS commanding officer was a stickler for everything in its proper place and dust free. I would fill out the correct form summit it to the desk clerk and retrieve the part. The yard was different. Items were under name and use. The code number was only used after the correct area was identified. Each row was a base with a MABS number. The base had a launch section and a recovery section. After the base was identified the containers were staged in installation need. Then after all that you use the code number to locate the correct container. I was lost trying to remember all the bases so after the first attempt I made a map on a three by five card that I kept with me. I enjoyed going out in the yard because I could find any container the quickest of anyone in our shop. One day I was directing a forklift operator moving containers around. I found a Honda 90 cc motor cycle stuck between two containers.

The motor cycle was old and wouldn't start but that didn't matter to me. I had a memory of riding a bike once but couldn't remember where. I had already forgotten camping with Morta. This memory seemed to bring pleasure as I admired the bike. This pleasure gave me the urge to fix the bike into usable condition. I located an empty container to act as a bike workshop. This container was twelve feet by eight feet and was located out on the edge of the graveyard. I now had a workshop and a project. I learned the history by asking questions around the unit about the bike. A Marine had left the bike in the yard when he rotated (transferred). I decided the bike was mine now, to justify my working on it. Rebuilding a bike in a box became my secret mission. I would work on it about one hour each day while on my breaks. I removed every part, ground it to bare metal rebuilt it, then painted it. I asked the other men in the MABS shop a lot of questions about what I needed to do. I would only ask one question per day per person in order to protect my secret. Rebuilding the bike helped me better under stand the functions of the absorber. The art of using parts or other objects never intended for that use developed as I worked on the bike. I found I could adapt the parts on military engines to replace parts I needed on the bike. The bike took me about a month to finish. It was now in good running condition, but what would I do with it? I was busy learning other things and soon forgot about the bike. The bike stayed in a metal box with all the other unused equipment in the supply acres.

My job in the MABS unit became like a part of me. I wanted to do it better and faster than anybody else does. I would try different approaches to assembling the absorber. Some ways worked faster some worked slower. I just kept learning more and more about my job, although I could not explain what to do without actually doing the work at the time that I was explaining. The names of parts and tools I could not remember, but the installation or function my memory retained. I picked up the habit of answering questions with a demonstration of what I would do. I was absorbed in the process of doing my job or helping other people do their job. I did every job I could just to learn. The common joke around the shop was I was trying to put the other Marines out of a job.

There was a Lance Corporal junior to me in grade by one week. Lance Corporal. Waitt always seemed to have an angry tone in his voice when he spoke to or about me. I didn't pay much attention to this type talk because it never occurred to me that it was mean. I assumed it was just his way of talking. But the best way to upset someone is not to realize they are trying to provoke you. One day I headed out to the supply yard to flag a large metal box to be transported into the shop. I was identifying code numbers. Smack! The side of my face was in pain. I flew to the ground and someone landed on top of me. I now could see it was Lance Corporal. Waitt pinning me down on the ground. He was hitting my chest and face with his fist. Each time he hit me he yelled, "You kiss ass son of a bitch." Waitt whaled the living hell out of me, then left. I lay motionless between the boxes for several hours.

The workday ended so the men were grouped in what is referred to as a muster. The Sergeant in charge calls your name and you answer back. I of course never answered when my name was called. The Sergeant sent two men to the back supply acres to look for me. They found me still lying on the ground with a bruised and bloody face. I was struggling to get to my feet by this time. The two men helped me up. I was sore and slow to move but I could walk under my own power. We went back to the building where I reported to the Sergeant. I washed the blood and dirt from my face while the Sergeant wrote the incident in the daily logbook. I was transported back to the barracks in a jeep that the Sergeant ordered to transport me.

I took a shower thinking I would clean up before going to chow. The pain from being punched and my tired state of mind suggested a short nap might help. The next morning was when I finally woke up. The pain was worse than the day before but I reported for work anyway. At muster that morning I received orders to report to the Commanding Officer. I got myself together as best I could and headed to the Commander's office after muster.

I stood in front of the Commander's desk at attention and stated "Sir Lance Corporal Macdonald reporting as ordered Sir." The Commanding Officer said "At ease," then went on to open the daily logbook and pointed at it. "Lance Corporal. Macdonald were you injured yesterday?" "Yes sir," I said. "Do you have anything you want to report?" the Commanding Officer asked. "No sir, I walked into a box on my own." The Commander then stated "When I was enlisted I walked into a few boxes myself. Do not retaliate against the box. Do you hear me?" The Commanding Officer stood up walked to the door and ordered me to follow him.

I followed one step behind and one step to the left of the Commanding Officer. We past through the administration office headed out the door. At that point the Gunny Sergeant started following a step or two behind me. The Gunny was the senior NCO (non-commissioned officer) in our MABS unit. The

Commanding Officer told me to be at ease and walk with the Gunny and him. I wondered what we were doing. I asked myself if these guys are going to take me out back for saying I walked into a box. The walk continued past the metal containers into the area referred to as the graveyard. I wasn't going down without a fight. I took every step prepared to attack as a defense against another whipping. The Gunny started, "We have a problem out here." Then the Commanding Officer started talking; "These decaying wooden spools are launch cables. We need to inspect and roll all one hundred and nine onto metal spools." In my mind defending myself started to be replaced with confusion. Why are they telling me this? I asked myself.

The Gunny looked at me straight in the eyes as if he knew the many questions darting across my brain. "You are the newest personnel in this unit," the Gunny said. "You show a hard continues work effort," continued the Gunny. The Commanding Officer interrupted what the Gunny was saying. "Lance Corporal Macdonald you learned to repair and rebuild absorbers in the short time that you have been in this unit." The entire situation at hand was happening different than I imagined. I knew what a launch cable was. I don't believe that personally I ever saw one. I couldn't grasp what was going on around me. A defense did not seem called for, but was it? I was confused. My mind kept asking myself "where am I "? The Commanding Officer continued talking as he started to walk back toward the shop direction. The last words from the Commanding Officer were "Gunny finish explaining the assignment".

The Gunny at that point started explaining the need of the launch cable. He went on to explain the tradition of the Marine Corps for only allowing the best supplies and equipment to aid our men in the front lines. That is when the Gunny got into talking about what the MABS unit job was. He explained about the need to thoroughly inspect each inch of each cable. We were looking for broken or rusted individual wires. A launch cable is made up of twenty-seven smaller cables weaned together. Each one of the twenty-seven cables is made up of nine wires weaned into a cable. A defective cable is if any seven wires are broken in any one-inch section.

The Gunny switched his conversation to wooden spools that were broken and decaying around us. His description about the spool condition was an understatement to say the least. My mind was working over time at being confused about life. I kept saying to myself "why me" but the Gunny was continuing to explain. He acted if, he knew that I understood what he was saying. My state of being mentally lost must have appeared that I understood the Gunny's explanation. I kept bobbing my head up and down every minute or so. The Gunny went on in his description about how tech reps. (civilian engineers) designed these metal spools to roll the cable onto. He walked over to some large metal wheels connected by a metal tube between them.

The Gunny was now standing next to the metal spool with his finger pointing to different features. This wheel the Gunny explained comes off by removing these five bolts. His finger touched each bolt. He then walked and stood between the two wheels of the spool to explain the tube. This tube comes out to fit through the center of the wooden spools so you can pick them up with a crane. Once you pick the cable up you place this four-inch solid metal ten-foot long rod through the center. The metal wheels go on the out side of the tube. You hold the whole assembly in the air with a forklift. Remove the crane unit and bold the wheels to the metal tube to complete the assembly. I looked at the Gunny still rocking my head up and down as if in agreement. I asked "Why me: I have no idea about any of this stuff".

The Gunny snapped me up against a metal box with the back of his fist. He bluntly stated "Marines follow orders. You do and die but you don't ever question". He ordered me to stand up then asked; "Did you understand what I said, how this assembly works?" I was in pain but I would not be defeated. I stood without reflecting any pain or emotion and agreed. The Gunny then started praising the way I performed my responsibility as a Marine.

The Gunny stood not a foot from my face and looked me straight in the eyes. The full glare and the power of a Marine penetrated my backbone. I was standing proud. I held my position by setting pain aside. I tried to understand what was happening around me. The Gunny started talking again "Lance Corporal Macdonald when you first started in my unit I thought you were a kiss ass looking for promotion. The longer you are in my unit the harder you are to figure out. You work to a standard better than could be expected from any Marine. You show a potential to be a good Marine. Then you go and do a stupid childish thing, grow up. Do a good job out here". That is when Corporal Kane walked over to where the Gunny and I were standing.

The Corporal was a big well-built Marine. I knew him from the shop area. This person was a lifer (someone in for twenty years) a kiss ass all the way. Corporal Kane was all Marine from his spit polished boots to the top of his shaved head. His only problem was he had no brain, or should I say his brain was the Marine Corps bible. "Corporal," the Gunny said, "This is the first member of your new crew, Lance Corporal Macdonald, work together." He went on to say "whatever you need, man power, equipment, you have thirty days and this mission will be complete." The Gunny left the area. The Corporal and I remained standing next to a metal spool.

I was in a causal relaxed mode, now the Gunny and Commander were gone. The situation was still unclear to me. I accepted what had happen as a normal life occurrence. I realized I was still learning and this was a lesson in life. In a friendly type of voice I asked, "OK Corporal what should I do." The Corporal decked (punched) me. He stood looking down at the ground where I was laying. "Your not my friend, your not my buddy, I am your Corporal, now get up and tell me what you need to get this job done." The Corporal's words raged in my ears as the pain in my face pounded with the beat on my blood rushing through my body. I attempted to ignore the pain as I stumbled to my feet. I felt the Corporal's hand grab the back of my collar and pulled me up.

I remembered the retired Marine telling me the best way to learn is to ask questions. The first day we spent talking to different Marines around the base from other units. Everyone we talked to told us a different way to do the job. The one consensus was not to let the cable unwind on its own. That consensus was the only fact I remembered from all the conversations that we had that day.

I did not understand what I was doing. I look back now, and the situation of my Marine Corps life reminds me of the saying "The blind leading the blind." I was trying to fit in with my friends, the Marine Corps, and/or just life. I had the total believe what was happening around me was normal. The flight from Hawaii and the Retired Marine kept reappearing in my thoughts. Is this amnesia for real or am I faking? I would have no memory about the Hawaii flight or any other thoughts. Someone would say or do something and certain thoughts would fill my head. I started to become aware of my memory loss. I was confused, but unknowingly learning a lesson from my stop in Okinawa.

I became aware that I could have this long technical conversation with others. The moment a conversation was finished I would not remember details. Sometimes I would not remember the subject of the conversation as we talked. I started questioning myself. Is everyone like this? Are other people covering up their not knowing things?

The flight from Hawaii gave me a lot of answers to the wrong questions in the rebuilding of my personality. I was still a developing child trying to fit in at a place I did not belong. I would ask myself many questions each moment of every day. A person answers questions with knowledge retained in ones memory. My catalog of information was growing. The problem was the pages were piling up on a desk in my brain without a clerk to properly file them. I learned to do jobs but could not remember that I knew how to do the job. I would just do jobs with the unknowing attitude that that is what everyone does. The flight from Hawaii and the disbelief of the men on this flight would be a tool to the development of my future.

The Corporal by the next morning put a complete crew together. We had a crane operator, forklift operator, and twelve crewmembers assembled at morning muster. The Corporal by the end of the second day had all the equipment assembled and men assigned to each job. I worked all day with the Corporal and had a change of opinion about him. I kept thinking about the phrase the retired Marine used "don't judge a book by its cover". This Marine may look like an Ox but he did his job in an all out follow the procedure motions. What the retired Marine had told me was reinforced with this one-day event.

The Corporal dismissed the men at evening muster. He ordered that I stay put. The two of us headed out to the graveyard. We surveyed the one hundred and nine decaying spools. We located the one in poorest condition. Our goal (as the Corporal put it) was to plan away to load the wooden spools with a metal spool. We worked and planned for the next four hours getting ready for the job at hand. The hardest part was visualizing placing the metal tube in without the cable coming off the wooden spool first. We came up with a plan that we thought should work.

The Corporal wanted to confirm the plan without the crew present. He informed me that my records show I was certified to operate forklifts and cranes. He then ordered me to get the crane from the shop. I had bounced off the metal box earlier for saying I did not know something. I jumped on the crane and started looking at the control panel. The Corporal thought I was doing a primary maintenance check before starting the engine. What I was really doing was trying to figure out how to start the engine. I must have turned or pushed the right button because the engine jumped. I went back pressing button that I had already pushed. After a few seconds the power of the diesel engine roared. The Corporal came over and slammed a lever back yelling, "You have the throttle to high". The two control levers were marked such as the cable up and down or the boom out and in. These labels made it easy to perform the right task called for at the time. I moved the levers slow when moving the cable incase something went wrong. Operating a crane came easy to me. I knew from that point on I could do anything I wanted to. My mind may not remember when talking or trying to explain but my confidence to do a job was building.

The spool assembly idea worked on the first attempt. The Corporal smiled as if to snub his nose at the Gunny. The Gunny was gone: Why was the Corporal signaling toward the shop with both middle fingers? I didn't ask. I shut down the equipment and got in the jeep that the Corporal pulled up beside me in. The next day at muster Corporal Kane's crew was dismissed from work and ordered to report back at 1700 hours.

The next twenty-six nights were hard work. I loved having a mission or goal to reach for. The Corporal had each night planned. We started with the spool in the poorest condition. The Corporal's belief was to go from bad to better. The men would be getting tired as the spool conditions got better near the end. This way the workload would be getting easier. It sounded good to me not that my opinion mattered.

The Corporal knew no mercy. He treated the men like animals. We had a mission to complete. The Corporal had a minimum number of spools per night to get done. The nights went from 1700 hours one day to 1300 hours the next day. The Corporal stood over the men barking orders, in a cruel manner. The men were like machines putting out top quality product for fear of the repercussions of a defect being noticed. My job was (what I now know as quality control) just solving problems that came up.

A questionable rust break in the cable would stop operations. I would be called to look at each break. What gave me the power to have such an important decision power? My back ground in understanding of what a cable was started only a few days earlier. I looked official with my metal pick. I would dig out the rust around each wire break. In every instance I would tell the Marine with the tar gloves on, to coat over the break. The number of other trouble shooting jobs kept coming up one after another. I was busy running back and forth to the graveyard helping load new metal spools in danger of coming unwound. A cable would snag or a machine would break. My job was to keep the operation moving forward. The Corporal followed me around continuously. He asked me questions when no one else could hear him. I never related his talk with me, to the way he was ordering the men to perform different jobs. I felt like the Corporal was reading my mind. I would be about to change a process or tell someone to do something but the Corporal would be one step ahead of me. Thoughts of how to change something or solve a problem would just come to me.

On the twenty-ninth day

we rolled our last cable to complete our mission. A new assignment was given to each Marine at morning muster that twenty-ninth day. The muster was being dismissed as the Commanding Officer and the Gunny walked up to the Corporal. The look on the Gunny's face suggested something was wrong. The three men stood talking for a few minutes. I was off to my next assignment.

Chapter eight: My First Offensive

The base went on full alert because of an offensive in Vietnam. Our Commanding Officer had the Sergeant call the dismissed men to attention so he could address the men. The Commanding Officer then informed us how the alert status took precedence over our activities. We were ordered to ship one complete air base out of the supply acres (nickname for an outside storage area where thousands of metal containers are lined up in rows) as top priority. The Commanding Officer, who was now facing the Gunny, stated, "You have seventy-two hours. Assign the men." The Gunny snapped to attention and saluted the Commanding Officer in robot-like motions. In a clear strong voice the words, "Aye, aye, Sir," bellowed through the air.

One by one, the men were assigned to squads. A squad is roughly about twelve men or any group of men under the command of a NCO. This NCO is usually a Corporal. Sometimes a junior grade Sergeant or less frequently a Lance Corporal, will be a squad leader. The senior-ranking Marine of the squad is always the leader. The squad is one fourth of a platoon. The Marine Corps calls for a Sergeant to be leader of a platoon except when one is not available. A large rotation of men during my second month left the unit with just one Sergeant and one Corporal. Most of the other men in the unit were now junior in grade to even me. I had no leadership experience or qualities that would make me even think of leading a squad. I was still building on my memory reservoir and trying to figure out--who was I? I was also trying to understand life and things happening around me. My name rang out as squad leader for the next group of Marines to fall in behind.

I was assigned to take my squad of men to Kadena Air Force Base five miles north of MABS Futema. Shocked, lost, bewildered, I was also impressed to be named squad leader. I stood tall and confident looking, but my mind was confused. Corporal Kane took me aside to brief me on my assignment. I was given a log-book and inventory sheets to manage the operation. The large metal containers would arrive at my staging area at Kadena. The job of my squad was to inventory every container before it was staged. The code numbers were to be checked off a master sheet. Then each code number was to be logged in a separate book. My squad had to have the staging area organized and secure with in ten hours. The C-5a cargo plane would land for the first load by that time.

A C-5a is a huge plane. A duce and a half-military truck can drive onto this plane turn around and drive off with out backing up. I had never seen a C-5a up to that point in my military career. The staging of the air base had to be coordinated between my squad and the Air Force personnel. They would be loading the plane under our direction. My job was to insure my men did their job and worked in unison with other military personnel. Corporal Kane went on to explain the loading process. The plane had to have the load placed so the first item off was the first used to install the new base. The cargo officer of the C-5a had to be involved in staging the load on the plane.

The last advice from Corporal Kane was about how to command. He said, "the person in charge has no friends." And he said "Take your feelings and emotions out of your body put them in a paper bag in your wall locker". This advice seemed to go against everything I have learned in the past couple years. I asked the Corporal, "Why would I do that?" I was looking puzzled. "You're a squad leader," out snapped these Marine-building words from Corporal Kane. He went on to explain a Marine could not command from his heart. Men get hurt and or die; that is the job. How can you worry about someone's feelings and not have it affect the efficiency of your command? To lead you have to push men beyond what is humanly possible. Feelings get in the way of a Marine doing his job. Corporal Kane's last words were, "You will understand better after the first day". I had the men load in the back of a duce and half for the ride to Kadena A.F.B.

The towns and roads that were usually filled with people, now stood empty. As we approached the main gate to Kadena, I noticed they were on full alert also. Maybe all the bases on the island were on alert? I noticed every person and piece of equipment were being used as we entered the gate. A jeep with a Lieutenant signaled us to follow them onto the taxiway. I clutched the clipboard with my paperwork, trying to remember what I needed to do. The more I thought, the cloudier my mind became. The jeep stopped a short time later on the edge of the grassy field. I jumped out of the truck to meet the Air Force Lieutenant headed my way. I snapped a sharp salute at the officer. He looked at me and casually raised his hand half way to his head as a salute back. At that point he gave me a map of the base and pointed to a red box penciled in. "This is your area where we are now," the lieutenant said. He went on to explain the way the trucks would come in and leave. How the movements of every vehicle had to be approved by the tower. He showed me where the plane would be parked and advised me to stage the cargo accordingly.

The tractor trailer trucks started rolling in as I was finishing assigning jobs to my men. There were two men at the entrance to the flight line. They stopped and logged the container numbers down. Tower clearance was obtained and the trucks moved up to the unloading area. Two Air Force forklift operators were added to my squad. Their job was to unload the trucks staging the containers and later load the plane. I had total responsibility? I kept asking questions because I had no idea how I got this job.

Staging the containers was similar to that in the supply acres back at the Futema MABS unit. I had learned the staging area at our unit so well this just fell into place. The art of using Marines to do jobs I could do myself was difficult. The pressure of controlling the twelve men under me grew as the delivery trucks started waiting to be unloaded. I found I could not do everything and that delegating authority made the job go a lot smoother.

After ten hours of hard work the fatigue became a factor in the continued success of the mission. I saw a need to reduce the number of men on site to allow sleep time. I could allow one third of the men to take one-hour naps at a time. This meant that after every three-hours of work, the men could sleep the fourth hour. The problem was quarters for the men to use on the Air Force base for sleeping. Plus the time it would take to transport them, the manpower and vehicles. I looked around and noticed an Air Force luggage trailer which had not moved since we arrived. I had the fork lift operator hook up to it and tow it next to my command area. The trailer had four empty luggage compartments to help support that my idea was correct. Each individual compartment could act as a sleep quarters per man.

I ordered the men as I saw fit to fill the time slots open for naps. The rotation continued through the entire offensive on an exact timing. Preventing any one from taking advantage or skipping naptime was the reason for my rigid timing.

The two Air Force operators I assumed were under flight line command. They worked hard at a fast pace just trying to keep up with the demand. I noticed the eyes of one of the operators getting tired. I ordered him into the nap time rotation. He objected not to the nap but when I ordered a Marine to operate his forklift. The Air Force dude told me, "No one is to touch my fork lift." I grabbed this man (who was about six inches taller and fifty pounds heavier than I was) by the throat. I had my thumb up under his jawbone. In one quick motion his head slammed against a container, and I yelled directly in his face. "This is my squad and my equipment and don't you forget it." I let the Air Force dude go as he was seriously gasping for air. He responded "Yes Sir!" and went into the sleep trailer.

The C-5a had landed but took two hours getting into loading position. Moving the huge plane around the flight line looked difficult. Planes and equipment had to be moved back from its path because of the size of this aircraft. Finally it stopped about fifty feet from our staging area. The tailgate opened as I expected it to, but when the cockpit started going up I was amazed. The bottom of the front part of the plane opened up, like the mouth of a large shark about to engulf its prey. The nose cone of the plane moved upward until the top of the cockpit windshield was perpendicular to the backbone of the plane. A wind tunnel formed that looked like some one removed the front and rear walls of the Empire State Building. One's imagination began to wonder how something so big could fly.

My job was to make the crew chief on the C-5a aware of which order the containers were to be unloaded at the receiving end. Loading the plane started as soon as the flight crew gave the clear signal. One forklift would bring container after container into the belly of the huge plane. The amount of equipment not only volume but weight was massive to be loaded on any one plane. I was busy attempting to be a leader to take the time to look into the plane, as it was now full. The forklift operator had stopped to watch the nose of the plane close. I walked up to the machine and ordered the operator to start loading the C-140 sitting beside the loaded plane.

The job was completed in the seventy-two hours allowed. The mission was successful. I felt tired and alone. The men who were also tired seemed reluctant to converse with me. I must have barked too many orders at them. There was a feeling of being alone even though there was others around me. One of the forklift operators approached me to shake my hand. He stated that I had done a good job controlling the events of the movement. Just before walking away he apologized for his attitude in the beginning about people operating his machine. I had no idea what he was talking about, but I smiled as I shook his hand. The men were now loaded on the truck for the trip back to Futema. At the main gate to Futema I was ordered to report to the Base administration office at noontime the next day.

Chapter Nine: Okinawa

I reported to the Base administration office at 1145 hours the next day as the Barracks NCO had ordered me to do. My transfer orders had been approved to leave Okinawa for West PAC command headquarters located in Iwakuni, Japan for reassignment. I was a little tired from working seventy-two straight hours, but excited to be headed for Vietnam. My orders stated to report to Iwakuni Japan for "disbursement," whatever that was. I applied for orders to Vietnam, so I thought that must be what the word disbursement means. I started the checking off the base process from MCAS Futema that afternoon. The process was the opposite from when I checked on to the base months earlier. I now knew my way around the base, which helped accelerate the process of checking out. The men working in most of these departments I now knew from helping them out or talking with them around the area. I practiced helping others because it kept me busy and gave me a way to talk to people that I did not know. My way of getting to meet people took many different forms. Mostly I met people because of my way of repairing different items with what was available. This was a great way to break the ice of when meeting new people. Helping different people on my part just kept increasing by others asking for help more often. First at my shop I fixed items when working on absorbers, then the barracks and eventually the base. I wasn't a repairman but if I saw someone needing help I would assist without question. I never wanted or took anything in return but people I helped seemed to remember me long after I forgot them.

My flight to Japan was due to depart Futema at 1400 hours the next day. This meant my last night would be spent packing, and cleaning for inspection before leaving. The time was about 2330 hours when I went down to the lobby for a soda. All the change I had was a nickel, which happen to be the price of a soda, but the soda machine ate my nickel without delivering a soda. A paper taped to the side of the machine was a list of people owed sodas from this machine. This list aggravated me and without thinking I placed my fist right through the machine display window. I removed a soda from the broken machine as a hand grabbed my shoulder from behind. I turned to defend my self-believing I was going to be nailed (punched). I lead with my fist as I turned and decked the person with one blow. I looked down and saw the duty NCO out cold on the floor. I quickly assisted the NCO by placing the cold soda can on his face to act as an ice pack. I then sharply slapped his face back and forth with my hand in the attempt to bring him around. I had witnessed this action on cartoon shows each Saturday morning so I assumed it was the right thing to do. The NCO's eyes opened, and I helped this unhappy Marine to his feet.

The NCO didn't understand the fact that I did not mean to hit him. I leaned him against a wall and held him up with my hand grabbing his shirt at his chest. At first he didn't seem aware of things happening around him. A few minutes later, I helped the NCO to the front desk where the duty NCO sits when not walking around the barracks. He seemed O.K. as we talked a few minutes before I picked up my soda and left the area. The NCO was upset about being punched, but didn't seem mad at me for doing it.

The next morning the barracks NCO, who was now on duty, ordered that I report to the Base

Administration office after breakfast. The Base duty officer appeared to be disturbed when I reported in to him, "Sir, Lance Corporal Macdonald reporting as ordered Sir." The duty officer picked up a logbook off his desk. He stood waving the book in front of himself. "Lance Corporal" his voice echoed in my ears, "You disrupted my watch." I started to speak but was ordered to speak only when told I could. I stood at attention for about fifteen minutes while this officer yelled and ridiculed me. He seemed to be stuck on the fact that I was going to be a private. My mind kept flashing to thoughts of the retired Marine at the Portsmouth Hospital. (Just do your job and the stripes will come back.) I could hear the duty officer's voice but it seemed far away as my mind was losing touch with reality. The duty officer's lips at that moment ever so slightly brushed my ear lobe. His words brought me back into the room: "Can you hear a word I am saying Private?" My morning only got more complicated as his voice rang in my ears.

I spent the entire morning at the base administration office. I sat as a child in a chair watching the parade of senior NCO's enter the door beside me. I could picture myself in my mind, marching down a gauntlet as my stripes were ripped from my collar and my body beaten. I sat motionless except for the movement of my eyeballs searching for answers from the movement around me. My eyes went back and forth identifying each movement in the room. "I will not give in; I am a Marine," my mind kept reminding me. The time for pain to be inflicted on me had come as a voice from the door ordered me into the room.

I stood front and center of the Commanding Officer's desk as the crowd of Marines present exited the room. The base commander sitting back in his chair explained the problem my indiscretion was causing. I was no longer a Marine stationed at his base. This meant that orders were needed from W-PAC (West Pacific Air Command) to return me to MCAS Futema base for disciplinary action. I would stay as a transient at the barracks until such time that my transfer was complete. At such time when the orders arrive I would be court marshaled for assaulting a duty NCO. The base CO ordered that I report to the Barracks NCO at 0500 hours each morning seven days a week. One missed or late check in I was told that would be my entrance into the brig until West-PAC answered. The room was now empty except for the two of us as the CO dismissed me.

I was now awaiting disciplinary action on four charges. The paper I was given stated that I was charged with assaulting a duty NCO, interference with a NCO's job, disobeying an order, and destruction of a soda machine. I had some decisions to make and a lot of writing before I forget what had happened. Writing notes in a book to remember things that I did became a habit after taking the letter writing course at El Toro Marine Air Base. The best place for making decisions would be back at the barracks. I could watch cartoons for help with deciding what to do. I didn't realize armed forces television was only on six hours at night and all day on weekends. While I was sitting at the television in the barracks, a NCO asks me why I was watching a blank television screen. I explained my situation. The NCO acquired a big smile on his face as if he was happy with my actions. When I finished talking he shook my hand and stated how that the man I hit deserved it. Someone was going to deck him sooner or later the NCO stated with a jubilant voice. Then the Marine explained how the barracks NCO's desk just received orders on my status.

The NCO explained how I was a transient and what the orders said that meant. My only requirement was that at exactly 0500 hours I had to sign the barracks logbook. The rest of the day was mine to do as I wished. After that, the NCO talked about how serious the consequences would be if I missed signing the book at the designated time. He then switched the subject to things to do on the island. Except for Kadena, my experiences were limited off the base. The NCO in some ways reminded me of the retired Marine in some of the things he talked to me about. The NCO kept telling me to see and learn everything I can because the Marine Corps is paying for this trip. Get off base and meet the people, enjoy how they live. Then you will appreciate what you have "back in the world" (That is what all military personnel refer to the United States as). We were interrupted by a disturbance that the NCO was called to. The last words he said were, "Enjoy your days as a transient because when that ends you're going to the brig."

I didn't want to sit around the barracks for days weeks or even months. I had not seen the island of Okinawa, so I thought why not take the NCO's suggestion? The idea of going to the brig registered in my brain, as if I was going to another country. It did not worry me because every day of my life was a new adventure. Why not the brig next? What the NCO had said made sense but I needed a plan because my money was limited. The first thought was about transportation. A taxi would cost too much. There was walking but that could limit my distance. That is when I noticed a Marine wheeling a pedal bike down the hall of the barracks. What about the

Honda 90cc sitting in a metal box at the supply acres? The bike was not registered but the plate from four years ago was still on it. I could change the last number of the year with some heat, a metal punch and a little paint. "Why not," I asked myself? Riding the Honda bike on base would be out of the question. However I could ride around the island and walk the bike while on the base.

My first day going off the base, I went to the northern end of the island. This was where a Marine grunt base called Camp Swab was located. I had never gone on this base because I never had a reason to. I knew however from talking to other Marines that Camp Swab was where foot soldiers practiced war games. The trip up to this base was going to be about forty miles one way. Up the only road that goes from one end of the island to the other made the trip seem simple enough. I started out on my adventure stopping at each town along my path. I found each town that I stopped in had unique characteristic qualities that sparked my interest. The trip was full of adventures. A woman who squatted over a banjo ditch (open sewer ditch) and took a pee while I was talking to her husband not five feet away. Some adventures were just talking to people. Most Okinawa people speak English along with their own language. The day was spent moving from one new experience to the next. I failed to realize that by this time afternoon had arrived. I was too busy to notice the time of day or even care. Streets were filling up with people doing their own thing. The vendors were trying to sell stuff to anyone they could snag. Young women were standing in front of bars saying "GI drink here, I make very happy." The one thing I couldn't get used to was when I had to stop the bike because of the crowds of people filling the street.*

Each time these woman in short mini skirts would walk up and squeeze my crotch and say, "Me make GI happy, two bucks." My mind was excited with all the interactions filling my life. I could feel myself turn red with embarrassment each time a girl touched me. The idea of young girls touching me between the legs caught me by surprise. Was this interaction normal? There was so much happening around me that the thought about girls touching me would pass until the next time it happen. The trip continued slowly from one town to the next because of the congestion. I finally reached the town nearest the main gate to Camp Swab. I just began to notice the late hour that it now was and set a time to start back toward Futema in my mind.

Every town I had seen appeared to be pretty much the same as all the other towns. People living and working in crowded conditions. I asked myself, Is this what life is like? Would live be like this after completing my tour in the Marine Corps? Skinny kids and adults eating what I would call pig food. The manner that these people ate even brought questions to me and I was a Marine. The Okinawa people stuffed rice and fish into their mouth with their hands. The local people kept squatting down to talk because they had no furniture. It would appear that at this late hour of the evening, most of the people walking around town were now American military personnel. I had seen the towns with few people on my way north and now on my return south the streets were crowded. I didn't anticipate the extra time it would take to travel back through the same towns to get back to Futema.

The crowded streets were so packed that at times I had to walk my bike in order to keep moving toward my objective. A clock was ticking in my head telling me I would be late for the 0500 check in. It was now approaching the wee hours of the morning, I guessed. I still had no idea the distance back to the base from where I was at this moment. There was only one main road north and south on the island, so I couldn't be lost. Futema had to be ahead of me, but at what distance? The slow travel confused me as to the distance that I might have traveled. The 0500-hour check in time was flashing across my brain. This was to be my first sign-in, and I would probably be late for it. I remembered some one telling me that life is predetermined: what is suppose to happen will happen. I kind of believed that because it was supported by the question I kept asking my self (Are people real or once they leave your site they don't exist). A military doctor explained my head injury to me by using those statements when I was at Portsmouth Navel Hospital. The doctor on several occasions sat down next to my hospital bed and explained how my loss of memory was a military experiment to test reactions of people. The doctor further explained how the military was trying to answer the question if people really existed when you could not see them. I to this day never forgot those conversations and still question reality? I looked down the road and there was MABS Futema's Main gate. I glanced into the guard shack as I walked my bike on to the base. The time was only 0400-hours I still had time. I was happy to leave the crowed streets behind and be back at the base.

The duty NCO logged me in on time. I signed the book and headed over to the mess hall. I knew the mess hall did not open for a half-hour, but I was friends with the cook. I could get a cup of coffee and wait outside. This gave me time to think of what I would do today. I only had a third of a tank of fuel left in the motor cycle. I could spend the dollar fifty to fill the tank, but my mission was to get free fuel from military vehicles. I decided to save my money and go to the southern end of the island and get back early enough to get fuel tonight. There was another American military base located past where I picked to visit on the map. In case I needed something. Now that my day was planned and I finished chow, I only had to clean my room and leave the base.

The delay in my transfer was a lucky break in ways. My mail would have been delayed a couple weeks before it reached my next base. The Marine who delivers the mail I had met months earlier when the strap on his mailbag broke. I fixed the strap with duct tape and a wire from the recreation room lampshade. The Marine delivering the mail was still using the same mailbag that I had repaired a month earlier. He seemed proud to talk about the duct tape repair with who ever asked. We became friends just to talk to when ever we see each other. He had been setting my mail aside to see if I was going to be delayed leaving the base because of the court marshal. I noticed in the mail that he gave to me a test had arrived for completion of my first college course. I was still taking courses through the mail with a goal of a college degree someday. Also in the mail that day was my Alton high school diploma. I had forgotten that was the reason I started taking these courses in the first place. I put the mail in my backpack to take with me on my trip. I felt lucky to know I graduated from high school. I wasn't exactly sure what high school was, but to graduate meant "Mission completed."

The travel distance to my destination was only about five miles south of the base on the same road I used last night. The streets were almost empty at this hour of the morning. Once reaching the area I was amazed at the peaceful beauty of the almost private setting on this crowded island. I found a flat rock on the edge of a beach to park my bike on. The day was sunny and hot as I sat on the rock looking at my mail from Alton. The town Alton kept my mind wondering these many questions. Where it was located? What it was like? Were the conditions in Alton the same as the villages I saw on Okinawa? The letters from my mother were my connection to a life I did not remember. I knew from the letters I had many brothers and a sister, but I did not recall a single fact about these people. The town of Alton that my mother talked about was as unknown to me as the people on the moon are to you. That sounds strange but reading my mothers letters was as if you are reading a book. You depend on your imagination and the belief the author is telling the truth. Also in my mail was several letters from a girl named Karyn. This was a summer resident of the church grounds in Alton Bay New Hampshire. Her Hometown was Exeter New Hampshire, which was located about thirty miles south of Alton. I remember receiving two or three letters from Karyn each week. I have no knowledge of when or where I met her. She was someone who I grew dependent upon for her letters. Karyn was an imaginary girl whom believed in me and would become my lasting link to survival. I did not and do not know where or when I met this girl. I remember having a picture of her that I used for support. The type of support that gave me a reason to believe life did exist outside the Marine Corps. I would some day after being discharged from the Marine Corps become close to Karyn. Each letter I received from Karyn made my memory retain thoughts of her. I would completely forget her existence until her next letter. Then a mad rush of facts would fill my head about her. A fisherman at that moment on the beach caught my attention as I watched him feed his net out to a buoy floating offshore. I watched for an hour or so while I wrote a letter to my mother and put some notes in my event logbook. In a desperate tug of war with pulling his net back in the fisherman was loosing the battle. I ran down to the beach with the belief this man needed help. Together we pulled the rope until the net appeared in the surf breaking at our feet. Seaweed made the rope slimy sliding through our hands. Pulling the rope was hard but when the net came out of the water there was about twenty-five good-sized fish in it. A boy appeared as the net cleared the water carrying a basket to collect the fish in. The situation seemed under control, which meant my job helping was done. I said good-bye and went back to the rock to finish my letters.

About an hour later the boy came to the rock where I had falling asleep and woke me up. He had some fins, masks, and snorkels with him. In broken English he asked me to go swimming with him. Off we went swimming through the coral reefs. We had a blast. We played games, chased fish, and swam in and out of the colorful rocks under the water. We swam late into the afternoon enjoying the warm water with all its beauty. We finally got out of the water looking like prunes as the water had wrinkled our skin. I was ready to head back to base to plan the next day's trip. The boy insisted I follow him to his house. Once there I enjoyed a great oriental meal with the boy, his father, mother, and sister. I had no idea what I was eating, but then again you don't know what you are eating at the mess hall either. I thanked the family in Japanese as I said good bye. I was slowly learning words in the Japanese language day by day. The problem was forgetting the correct way to pronounce the words or just what the words meant. My lack of memory effected my daily life but I was not aware that I had a problem.

I arrived back at the base early in the evening, did what I had planned and went to bed. At 0430-hours the duty NCO rapped on my door to advise me of check in time. This was a whole new day. Today I wanted to go east over the mountain toward the Navy base. The distance on the map was only an inch, but there was a mountain in the way. Traveling on a winding country road established in my mind the existence of an unpopulated side of the island that I had no idea existed. I got about halfway down the backside of the mountain when I saw some horses grazing in a small field. I stopped to check things out and maybe learn something. My mind had accepted Okinawa as a crowded dirty place, but this was open farmland. I thought, what a place to get away from the base. I parked the bike, so I could stand and admire the horses. I took the bungie cords of the back off my bike to try an idea I had that would aid me in riding a horse. After catching one of the horses I hooked one cord to each side of the horses halter. This made a crude type of reins so I could control the horse. I rode this well-mannered horse for what must have been a couple hours. Up and down the trails enjoying everything around me. I saw a part of Okinawa that was impressive, to say the least. The five other horses that were in the pasture followed us the entire time, every place that we went. We were like a Marine squad on patrol, scouting out the countryside. The birds and other animals were the enemy. We secured the mountainside by scaring off the invaders. All of a sudden we were captured. The enemy had a secret weapon that blocked the path. The owner of the farm found us and was mad because I was riding his horse. I released the bungie cords allowing them to fall to the side of the horse's head and dismounted.

My Japanese language was limited but I did learn to speak enough to have a conversation in a basic way. My first job was to settle the farmer's down. He was talking so fast I could not understand a word that he said. After a few minutes of my repeating "Just a minute," in Japanese, he stopped talking. Then I walked back to the farmhouse with him, as he insisted I do. By the time we arrived at this man's home we were talking as friends. I agreed that shoveling manure out of the barn would be my payment for my use of his horse. I enjoyed the work, but the smell was enough to gag you. The completed job only took one hour. The farmer who was pleased with my work for which he tried to pay me one yen (one third of a penny) as I walked to my bike. I couldn't understand a word he said, as the farmer began speaking fast again. I was not sure what he was trying to say, so I decided to relax a few minutes with him.

I grabbed two sodas from my backpack, which was resting on the seat of my bike. If I had driven another hundred feet on the rode none of this would have happen. My bike was parked that close to this man's house. Anyhow, we ended up sitting on the front porch of the farmhouse. The barn appeared more livable than his house was. We talked, if you want to call what we were doing communication. I was trying to ask why he didn't spread the manure around his farm. Finally the farmer stood up and pointed to a missing link on the apron that pushes the manure out to the spreader. While drinking our sodas, my eyes were searching for something to fix this mans machine with. I focused in on the S shaped hook on the end of my bungie cord that was hanging from a tree. I took the S hook and bent it several times connecting the two ends of the apron together with it. The farmer was so happy he started talking a mile a minute again, so I couldn't understand him any more. The evening hours were setting in as I thanked the farmer and got up to leave. I left the two-bungie cords hanging from the tree as I walked to my bike. I thanked the farmer again and headed back to the base.

The next day Steve was off work and wanted to show his swimming hole to me. Steve was deeply in love with an Okinawan girl, so when Steve was off work the two of them did everything together. Today she was working at home, which meant Steve was free. Steve and I rode on my bike to the swimming place that day. We ended up just north of Kadena, AFB deep into some woods, a beautiful place to be. A stream of water was falling about sixty feet off a rock ledge. A pool about twenty feet in diameter carved outs of solid rock caught the falling water. The water was so clean you could see deep down to the rock bottom of the pool. We swam for several hours, each taking turns diving off the ledge from where the water came. The whole time I felt this place was familiar to me as if I had been here before. I had a warm comforting feeling about being here. I knew these feeling were confused because the only place I had been swimming while on Okinawa was the reefs. Steve had to meet his girl friend so we headed back to the base after only swimming a few hours.

At the base before Steve left he wanted to have a talk with me. What he said to me was strange at the time but something I would think about quit often in the future. Steve started talking about friendship and how he noticed I did not have my own personality. He told me that every time I met someone new, I started talking and expressing myself like that person. I needed to be myself, not what I saw in other people. I told Steve I would try to see for myself what I was doing. I was asking myself questions all the time. Now I had a new set of questions to ask. I was always confused at what to do about everything in my life. Understanding what Steve was saying started me thinking about this subject. I didn't know my personality was missing. Could I find it? What if I did not find it?

I spent the next ten days walking my bike on and off base. I visited north and south, east and west on the island. I worked and played with different native people each day. I was having trouble remembering day to day events. I kept writing notes in my memory log book but since I never repeated doing things the events slipped away from my mind. I continued writing a paragraph on each new event in letters to my family back in the States, as that was a habit I formed. I was also trying to keep up with my correspondence courses along with everything else. The more I did, the more exhausted I got, which meant the more that I forgot things. Soon I was having trouble remembering if I had eaten or not. I took a couple days to relax and never left my room. The duty NCO would bring the logbook up to me and make me sign in each morning. Slowly my mind was asking who am I? And what am I doing here?

After resting, I spent the next week hanging around the barracks writing about everything I could think of. One day my friend from the MABS unit asked me why I wrote so many letters and who to?

Actually, I wrote very few letters, just one to my family each week. The fact that this friend was asking questions about my letter writing did not make since to me, at the time. My response to him was that I like to write. I did this just to hide my not understanding what he was talking about. He assumed my correspondence courses and notes were letters, I guess. After a short conversation, he described how he mentioned to his sister, in one of his letters about me. His sister who was a Texas cowgirl, liked what she heard. The letter he was holding in his hand described how she wanted to write to me as a friend. I wrote a letter to her that day as a way to make a new friend. The day her answer back arrived was the day of my disciplinary hearing.

I cleaned up my appearance with a haircut and starched uniform along with spit shining my boots. I reported to the base commander's office fifteen minutes before the time my orders read. The door opened in front of me as I approached it. I stepped to one side and snapped to attention. The base commander came out, followed by the MABS warrant officer, Gunny and Corporal Kane. Corporal Kane was now a Sergeant. The base commander stood with his back to me as the others walked past him. I was ordered after everyone was gone to stand front and center of the desk by the base commander. "Sir Lance Corporal Macdonald reporting as ordered." I said standing at attention in front of his desk. "Corporal," the base commander said. "I have never done this before. Promoted a Marine who deserves to be court-martialed for the trouble that you are in". He started saying, "If your superiors vouch for you the way they just did, you are the type Marine we need in the Marine Corps." Then he made the statement to me that so many others have told me before and since: "grow up." The base commander called me to attention and shook my hand with a sturdy grip. My rank at that moment became official as a Corporal in the United States Marine Corps. He placed his face right in front of mine. In a clear cold voice he told me my flight for Iwakuni Japan would leave in one hour. "Be on it." he ordered "Dismissed".

I flew on a C-117 cargo plane from Okinawa to Iwakuni, Japan that day. I was the only person on the plane besides the pilot. "Corporal," the pilot said as I got on the plane, "It's going to be a short trip. If you want to ride up front in the cockpit you can." Smiling from ear to ear, I followed the pilot into the cockpit. The cockpit had instruments, gauges and levers, so many looked like too much for any one man to keep track of. My head was spinning with joy as the plane sped down the runway. In the cockpit you can feel when the front wheels leave the ground, as the plane becomes airborne. The plane goes into a graceful slide as everything on the ground disappears out side of your sight through the plane's windshield. You see the clouds floating in the air approaching the plane at a quicker and quicker pace as the plane reaches altitude. You feel the vibration of the engines slightly caressing your body through the seat. The headset that you wear in the cockpit removes all sound, except for conversations between pilot and tower personnel. The loud noise and uncomfortable ride reminded me each time that I still did not like the C-117 plane. This trip was exciting because I was in the cockpit. I was, in a way, the co-pilot of this flight, sitting beside the pilot.

The pilot pointed through the windshield to an island off in the distance. "That is Japan," he said. I watched as the land mass ahead, which grew in size the closer we got. The pilot again pointed his finger to the land approaching. I could now see the runway starting to take shape. The pilot started talking to the Iwakuni tower about landing directions at the same time that he was directing me to look in the direction of his finger pointing out the windshield. In a change of his actions the pilot began moving levers and tapping gages on the dashboard with his fingernail. A red light about the size of a dime started blinking. The worst sound to me in a cockpit is when the pilot says, "Whoops!" Frantically, the pilot started moving different buttons trying to get the red light to go out. The pilot spoke to tower warning of possible right landing gear up. The tower spoke back with directions and attitude that brought us in a path past the tower about one hundred feet above the ground. Tower confirmed no right landing gear to the pilot.

"Prepare for a emergency landing!" rang out over the radio waves. Lights began flashing at different points on the ground below. Yellow trucks raced down the taxiways to take up their designated positions. The pilot now relaxed, acting as if crashing was a routine event. This was exciting to me as my body's reactions started to demonstrate my excitement. I had a smile on my face looking in every direction as fast as my eyes could move. Riding in a cockpit, then crashing, what could be more adventuresome? The pilot reached over and jerked my seat belt tight with a force that startled me. His words of sarcasm were mocking my happy attitude about this situation. The thought of getting hurt or dying never crossed my mind. (I was too young to die) I had watched a plane crash before while landing at El Toro and wondered what it was like. Now I'm doing what I only dreamed about from the ground. The activity on the base below was getting closer as we approached the runway on final.

The plane's wheels started to touch the runway with the pilot calmly sitting beside me snapping switches off. Wheels started screaming as if in pain as they skipped off the runway surface. A jolt in the motion of the plane indicated the deployed wheels were firmly on the ground. The pilot leaning sharply to the left side of his seat looked like he was holding the plane's right wing in the air. I quickly started leaning to my left to help. Just before the plane came to a complete stop the right wing touched the ground. Out of the side of the cockpit window you could see sparks snapping from the wing tip. The plane came to a complete stop in the middle of the runway tipped to one side.

The pilot undid his harnesses, (mine I had undone before we stopped) and jumped out of his seat. He grabbed me by the back of my collar and pulled me to the exit door as I scrambled to keep up with him. He let go of me long enough to open the door. He then pushed me out of the plane, not caring that the first step was ten feet down to the ground. I managed to jump as I left the plane for the ten-foot drop into a sea of white foam. Covered in foam from head to toe the pilot guided me to the side of a yellow truck. This truck had a gun mounted on top shooting white foam covering the plane and anything else in its path. The pilot had a quick conversation with one of the firemen after which he guided me to another vehicle. We then sat on the tailgate of a fire rescue pickup truck for a lift to the flight operation's building located on the flight line. The pilot went into the building leaving me standing in a lost state of mind.

I was soon directed to a gray pick up truck that contained my duffel bag. I got a ride across base to the administration office so I could check in. The base looked different from Futema. There seemed to be more open space and smaller buildings, but more of them. We soon arrived at the administration office that was located near the main gate to the base. The first thing I did when I entered the building was to change into a dry uniform. Then I filled out a transfer form as the retired Marine instructed me to do. A sergeant at the desk looked at me in a strange way when he noticed the form. The words, "Corporal, how would you like to go to Portsmouth Naval Station?" came from his mouth. The Sergeant explained the situation that a Corporal was needed by the Military police to escort a prisoner to the brig. They had been waiting for my transfer for days now from Okinawa. I had no idea what he was talking about. All I knew is Marines don't ask questions, they complete their mission. I was directed by the Sergeant of the administration office to the MP shack to receive my orders and equipment.

The MP sergeant had me signing forms with in a few seconds of my entrance. A forty-five-caliber hand gun, a holster, and ammo belt were handed to me. The next thing I knew, I was in a jeep with an MP Lance Corporal driving. The direction we traveled was back to the flight line where I had just came.

Once we arrived on the flight line a jeep with three Marines in it met us. A Corporal got out and told me to follow him before I could take possession of the prisoner. As we walked toward a building the Corporal told the driver from my jeep to guard the prisoner. We entered the flight line operations building to sign more papers. I had no idea what was happening, but the desk Sergeant wrapped a yellow band around my arm that had big red letters MP on it. While in the building a non-stop chain of orders and information was given to me. I was told I had priority on all flights to Portsmouth Naval Base. The prisoner was my responsibility, if he escapes I would have to serve his time until he is captured. The travel time allotted was fifteen days maximum, I was told. I was then handed my orders in writing that we had just discussed. And I was handed a copy of everything I had signed as we walked back to the jeeps.

The Marines who were guarding the prisoner got him out as we approached. They walked in front of us to the foot of the steps that lead into the plane. One of the MP's once we were at the foot of the plane handed me some keys and made the comment, "He's your prisoner now." I helped the prisoner up the stairs and buckled him to his seat. I then did the same for myself so we were in side by side seats. The plane started taxiing down the runway on its way to Tokyo for our first stop. I was now an MP transporting a prisoner. It felt unreal- what was reality. Anyway?

I was lost in my own mind. In my possession was a carry bag containing my shaving gear and a change of underwear that I quickly grabbed from my duffel bag. I was wearing my fatigues (work uniform) and a starched cover with a loaded pistol strapped to my side. My mind was trying to catch what reality is. Were the questions darting across my brain rational questions? Was this normal life? I asked myself, who am I? I was told in Okinawa I would be going to the brig for hitting a NCO. Now I am escorting someone else to the brig. I got promoted instead of busted to a lower pay grade at my disciplinary hearing. One minute I am headed to Japan then the next minute some place else. I have a travel route to Portsmouth Naval Base time and flights all planned. I sign a paper and another Marine gives me three hundred dollars cash. He tells me it is all the travel money I will get. I had many questions as I sat on the plane quietly looking around, but what were the answers? Since the accident in New Hampshire I learned to accept what was happening to me as real. I had built a trust to believe that what people told me was true unless I knew it was not. My understanding was different though. I could remember short pieces of past experiences, but they did not answer my questions. Was this a part of a military medical experiment that the doctor in the hospital explained to me? Was this a test to see if I remember not to ask questions? These Marines in the administration office told me that they were waiting for me to arrive from Okinawa. Marines do or die, I had received orders for a mission. Now I must complete the mission.

The C-117 landed in Tokyo only to have the prisoner and I walk directly to a plane ready to leave Japan for the United States. A conversation soon started after take off when my prisoner asked if I had a cigarette. I never did smoke so I leaned across the aisle and asked the girl smoking if I could have one of hers. After the girl handed me a cigarette, I turned my attention back to the prisoner. The prisoner was a nice person. He had a wife and a one-year-old child living in Wyoming waiting for him to complete his time in the Marine Corps. That wait was now going to be for three to seven years longer. Alcohol was the cause of his problems. So many Marines drink excessively as their way to escape their daily life. I personally could not see how anyone could afford the cost of drinking that much. We all got paid the same, but I never seemed to have extra to waste on booze or cigarettes.

The prisoner described to me how he was drunk when he met this young man on the bench at the base golf course. The time that night was only about nine o'clock but that is where he liked to go on nice nights to write his wife a letter. It was common for him to bring a bottle of whiskey and drink while writing. A short time latter this particular night another young man came by and they started talking. They drank the bottle of whiskey together "then it just began" the prisoner said. The two men ended up performing a sexual act together. The young man's father came for a walk at the golf course and they were caught in the act. It turned out the young man was the base Master Sergeant's fifteen year old son. The thought of how this was the time my feeling belonged in a paper bag skipped through my mind. I was a Corporal in the Marine Corps whom had a mission to complete. I continued talking to the prisoner, but I no longer felt sorry for him. I had no feelings one way or the other. I had a direction and/or purpose to guide me, which meant my mission came first.

The next stop was in Anchorage, Alaska, I thought as questions of time and location entered my mind. This would be a long ten to thirteen hour flight at which time I would not able to sleep because of my responsibility to guard the prisoner. On guard duty at El Toro I learned never to sleep while standing guard. Our layover when we arrived in Alaska we were told would be three hours plus. On this long flight I watched the prisoner sleep as I sat quietly so as not to disturb him until finally we landed.

Food seemed a good way to fill some of the time and keep us busy in order to stay awake. It had been a while since we ate our last meal on the plane and I had three hundred dollars in my pocket. I wasn't sure if I could spend it for food or not. The prisoner assured me that the money was mine to spend as I wish. He went on to explain the purpose of the money was to pay for expenses, to and from Portsmouth. Food served at the airport was a lot better than the mess hall the prisoner explained. The next thing I knew we were enjoying talking and eating as the time passed at what seemed a slow pace. It only took us one hour to eat the meal. What next I asked? The clock on the wall showed we had about two hours before getting back on the plane for the next part of our trip. We started walking around when the prisoner spotted a lounge and asked to go in and sit down. He convinced me it was the guard's responsibility to get the prisoner a drink before he entered in to the brig. Sitting in the lounge for ninety minutes started the prisoner talking about everything on his mind. He mentioned I should have a drink with him and relax. He explained how it would make me feel better. I drank just soda because each time he mentioned drinking the private on guard duty at El Toro appeared in my mind. A Gunny Sergeant from El Toro was now a private because he got in trouble for drinking on duty. I did not need to waste money to get into trouble. It would find me on its own. I stuck to drinking soda. Before we left the plane a stewardess requested we be at the gate thirty minutes before the other passengers boarded the plane. We left the lounge and then Alaska on time for our next stop at Chicago.

The next stop was Chicago what people on the plane was calling the Windy City. I asked the girl sitting next to me if she knew where Chicago is located? She introduced herself as Beth. I watched her eyes roam up and down my uniform, time and time again. She focused in on the pistol and MP strap as she was talking. I learned her home was in Ohio before she got to telling me about Chicago. She described where Chicago was and that she had been there many times. Beth and I talked for about an hour in a friendly manner. The next thing I knew Beth had fallen asleep on my shoulder. The prisoner had fallen asleep shortly after take off from Anchorage, leaving me attempting to stay awake as I sat there. The pilot woke everyone on the plane up when he announced over the speakers we would be landing in Chicago in twenty minutes. This got Beth scrambling to get some paper and a pen out of her purse to write her address and phone number on for me. She handed it to me holding my hand while she asked a question. In a soft voice with her eyes becoming moist, she asked "Will you stay with me for a couple days on your way back?" We landed at Chicago only long enough for the people departing to get off. Beth kissed me on the cheek before leaving the plane. The plane soon after departed Chicago airport. We were headed to Boston in a very short time.

The plane ride to Boston didn't seem that long; my mind was busy. I was thinking of Beth the entire flight. I knew my visit with her would be fun. I was planning on maybe going to visit her for a day or so. The prisoner got to talk on the subject of how sweet Beth was on me. I didn't think sweet was the correct word but she was fun and it was nice to think about visiting her. The prisoner insisted I "think about the stop" because I would be crazy not to visit her. He then went on to describe how the Marine Corps gave me fifteen days travel for situations like this. They (the Marine Corps) know a Marine may need a woman after completing a mission, the prisoner stated. I had no idea where Ohio was, but I could stop there for a short time. It was on my return route, I was told. I had directions, her invitation, and her phone number. I agreed with the prisoner that I would stop and visit Beth on my return trip. The plane landed in Boston on time with no problems. We were first to board on the plane at all stops and last to get off the plane when we landed.

Two Marine Military Policemen met us at the gate in perfect Marine form. Dressed in formal uniforms with shinny brass buckles and spit-shined boots standing at attention. They positioned themselves one on each side of the prisoner for the walk through the airport. I walked behind as I watched the three Marines walk in step with each other. The MP's refused to adjust their position to avoid on coming people in the airport terminal. No one was allowed to walk near the prisoner at any time. Eventually we got into a gray military van parked in a no parking zone in the road out side of the terminal. The ride from Boston to Portsmouth Naval Base seemed longer than the plane ride from Chicago. Riding in a cage with no windows listening to the vibration of the medal walls was nerve racking. The two Marine MP's were spit polished hard core men of steel. They sat at attention on the entire trip with out any unnecessary movement. The ride only lasted one hour as we entered the main gate at Portsmouth Naval Base but dark had fallen by now. The two MP's escorted us to the Sergeant of the Guard's desk in an almost machine like fashion. They stood at attention until put at ease by the Sergeant sitting at the desk. I placed my paper work on the desk and asked the Sergeant to sign the paper work where it was called for. He pulled several pages out of the pile and signed them. At that point I handed the Sergeant the keys to the handcuffs and the two MP's escorted the prisoner away.

The Sergeant assigned me a place in the Marine Barracks to clean up and get some sleep. This was a room with a bed, a private bathroom, and a washer and dryer in it. I took a shower and washed my uniform and underwear along with me during this process. I was wearing the only uniform I had with me on this trip and it needed to be cleaned for my return trip. It cost fifty cents to use the washing machine, but the dryer was free. I put my uniform in the dryer after putting my clean dry underwear on. I slept for about an hour. The next thing I remember was waking up from the alarm on the dryer telling me my clothes were done. I starched and ironed my uniform with the items provided for that job located in the room. The cover (hat) I had been wearing was still starched and stood strait up as called for in Marine protocol. I felt a lot better than when I arrived at this base a few hours earlier. Now I was clean and ready for the day's events. My mind lost track of reality. I forgot where I was, or what I was. My mind was a blank I sat for a minute in the attempt to figure out where I was? I had no memory of my location in the world. Eventually I remembered about the Marine Corps, and reported back to the Sergeant of the guard in the guard shack. I was ready to be transported back to the airport. The Sergeant ordered the MP over the radio to pick me up from where ever they were, to transport me back to the airport. I was excited with the thought of visiting Beth in a place called Ohio as thoughts of her kept flashing in my mind.

I caught a flight from Boston to New York on a stand by status with no trouble. A stewardess told me that in New York I had to switch airlines to complete the trip to Ohio. I sat beside this pretty blonde girl on a plane that had only a few other passengers on it. We started talking soon after take off from the runway in Boston. Her name was Cathy, and she was from a small town in Indiana. I felt relaxed like we had been friends for a long time. I just enjoyed being with Cathy. We became friends in that short flight from Boston to New York. The flight did not last long enough in my mind. Cathy asked me to fly to Chicago with her because she thought her mother would approve of me. I could spend the next couple days with her and her mother before heading back to Japan. She lived about five miles south of Chicago just over the Indiana State line. I forgot completely about Beth and went with Cathy to Chicago to stay with her for a couple days. *Her mother met us at the gate in the terminal as we got off the plane. I liked her mother form the first words she spoke. During the drive to Indiana a bond developed between Cathy and me. Cathy and her mother looked almost identical as if they were twins. Both girls had long blonde hair and a baby doll face. Their bodies were slim with huge breasts pushing out of the sweaters. The evening was late by the time we arrived at their house, so without much talk we all went to bed. On the next morning Cathy and I walked all around her hometown talking to each of her friends that we met. In the afternoon Cathy started complaining that I would say and do the most immature things. She told me I was a baby trying to play Marine and that I should grow up before I got in trouble. I had the idea form in my head that I wanted to leave. If Cathy didn't appreciate my personality, in my mind this meant she didn't want me around. I had to think about not changing my personality to that of people I meet, just to fit in. I went to her house got my things and hitched hike to the airport with no discussion on my part with anyone. I got to the airport in time to catch a flight to Anchorage, Alaska with no waiting time at the terminal. I slept the entire flight until the stewardess woke me up after the plane had landed. All the other passengers had departed the plane and the stewardess were cleaning up when they found me in the seat sleeping.*

My priority flight status for getting on planes did not work without a prisoner. I was told to wait for the next available seat on any flight headed in my direction. While sitting in the waiting area I watched this man wash the windows that looked out of the terminal onto the runway. I got out of my seat after a period of time and just started helping this man wash, move ladders and the staging around to different areas. We worked for about two hours together when the man shook my hand and said his workday was done. We had been talking as we worked so this man knew why I was stuck waiting for a flight at this airport. He let my hand go as he invited me to dinner at his house to meet his wife.

I felt good that Jake (the window washer) wanted me to meet his wife. We watched her through the door window before entering his house. I learned this mans wife's name was Moo as we stood watching her. What a colorful perky lady she was as she bounced around her kitchen dancing and singing preparing a meal. She was a bit overweight but I bet she could handle herself in any situation that came her way. The noise of the door opening made Moo stop her actions and turn to greet us. Dinner was served soon after we arrived. Moo sat her husband Jake down and replaced his shoes with slippers before we could start eating. The entire process of every thing Moo did was to please her husband. Jake in return did things to please Moo, such as hold her chair or help pour the milk. The meal contained enough food to feed ten men and still have left over for another meal. I am not sure what the meal I ate consisted of but the taste made the food melt in your mouth. I wanted to eat more but I was too full. The meal was that good that you couldn't get enough. I thanked Moo for such a pleasant experience of meeting her and being allowed to enjoy her cooking. I told her I would never forget her but that I had to catch a 2200-hour flight to Tokyo. Jake dropped me off at the airport just in time to catch my flight to Japan. I only remember one part of this flight. Learning that the unofficial name for escorting a prisoner was called a "Brig rat chaser. I landed in Tokyo the next day after completing the long flight back to Japan. I then caught a C-117 to Iwakuni, Japan for my next duty assignment.

One Marine Military Policeman on the flight line driving a jeep stopped at the plane. The PFC never said a word the entire time I was with him. I got in the jeep and he drove me back to the guardhouse where all this brig rat chaser duty started less than a week ago. A lieutenant ordered me to surrender all my military police equipment. He then asked in a demanding voice, "Corporal do you have a Military Police MOS (job) title? I stood at attention because I had no idea what he was talking about. The lieutenant went on as he told me the rules that I had disobeyed during my deceptive actions. All I knew was I was in trouble again, awaiting disciplinary action for impersonating an MP.

The next day I reported to the Sergeant at the guard shed to be informed about the disciplinary action to be taken against me. The Sergeant on duty explained to the Lieutenant and myself how a Corporal was being transferred from Okinawa. This Corporal was to be assigned to escort the prisoner on his way to his new duty station at Portsmouth Navel Base. The Corporal was two days late when I arrived from Okinawa. It was assumed I was the Corporal that was in route to Portsmouth Naval Shipyard. After a discussion between the Lieutenant and the Sergeant about the mix-up the Sergeant walked away. The Lieutenant through the disciplinary paper work in the trash and dismissed me. The sergeant stopped at a desk and ordered the PFC to drive me to the MABS unit located on the flight line.

The Lieutenant stopped me, as I was about to go out the door. His questions confused me. He talked about how he read in my file and learned I was from New Hampshire. He wanted to know why I didn't go home while I was in New Hampshire. I responded that I went to Portsmouth Naval station not NH. I had no idea the base was in New Hampshire, never mind thirty miles from where I grew up. I was confused but began to accept the fact I may never understand why I am unable to understand so much. I did question to myself why the Marine Corps wasted so much time on disciplinary action?

Chapter Eleven: Runway leadership

I caught a jeep ride to the MABS unit located on the flight line. The building I noticed as we approached it had a red sign with yellow letters that read MABS and the unit next to the building number. This sign identified the building as my next duty work unit. The building it self was a two story metal structure, a typical military style building. The width of the building was only eighteen feet but the length must have been almost one hundred feet. There was a large garage door at one end facing the runway. The area around the building was empty except for a gray Chevy pickup truck parked near the entrance door. The driver stopped the jeep on the backside of the building near another door. I removed my duffel bag from the jeep and set it by the door to the building.

I entered into a small room with four desks stationed in box formation around the area. There were four Marines reading papers while occupying a desk each. The bright colored walls and shining metal objects caught my attention. Everything was positioned and in an organized fashion at designated locations. The extra chairs were all equal distance from the side of each desk. A wastebasket, which was located on the opposite side from the chair, was a precise six inches from each desk. On the desktops was books lined up one half inch from the front edge left side forming a strait line. The row of books ended near the center of the desk where a nameplate identified the Marine located at that desk. Across on the left side of the desk was a reading lamp of shining brass stock. I saw a Gunny Sergeant stand up at the desk nearest the back corner of the room. This Marine's appearance was as spit shined as the room.

The Gunny with his tough Marine Corps posture shook my hand and welcomed me into the unit. "Welcome Corporal. We need a NCO for a runway crew. You do know how to operate the gear?" he asked. I thought to myself, I have never seen the gear used that I know of, but why say anything? (My memory since the accident was such that even if I had seen the gear operated, chances are that I would not remember.) The Gunny introduced me to the other three Marines in the room before we passed through the door behind the Gunny's desk.

The door was marked with a sign, "Unit Commanding Officer." A single knock on the door was answered with the word "enter". "Captain this is Corporal Macdonald" the Gunny said. The Captain stood up behind his desk and shook my hand. He welcomed me into the unit with the regular pep talk. I had heard this pep talk many times before. It always sounded as though this talk was Government Issue words for officers to say. (We run a tight unit here keep out of trouble and do your job.) The Captain went on speaking, "This is a quiet unit and I want to keep it that way." He then asked me if I understood. "Yes, sir" I responded as the Gunny and I then left the room after being dismissed.

Next we went up these narrow stairs to the second floor of the building. There were rows and rows of shelves stuffed with packages. I couldn't remember the names of the parts to the absorbers, even though I could rebuild them. The absorber is a brake unit located in a pit on the each side of the runway. The two absorbers are connected by a wire rope that runs across the runway. Together these absorbers stop fighter jets in a short distance by catching a tail hook that is connected under the tail of the plane. At least in my mind I thought I knew how to rebuild an absorber. I couldn't even remember how to describe how to take an absorber apart to rebuild it at that moment. I picked up a package off one of the shelves as I walked down the row following the Gunny. My mind clicked and I recalled where this part was located in the absorber assembly. A picture formed in my mind as if I was working on an absorber. This part I thought to myself, very seldom needed to be replaced if ever I thought. On the shelf there must have been four hundred of these parts. Why, I asked myself would you store this many parts in one place? I continued looking on more of the shelves as the Gunny and I continued our trip down the aisle. My mind was like a catalog book flipping the pages. I could not recall anything to do with an absorber as I walked. Then each time I saw a part a page in my mind opened up and described where it went. We reached a desk in the rear of the room, where a Lance Corporal was filling out paper work.

"Lance Corporal," the Gunny said as he introduced the two of us. The Gunny went on to inform the Lance Corporal I was to be assigned leader of a runway crew. The Lance Corporal stood strait as an arrow while talking to the Gunny. I kept looking around the room amazed I could remember different parts and not recall if I could rebuild and absorber or not. Soon the Gunny was moving us toward the stairs to exit the supply room. The last words I heard the Gunny say was, "Have you spent the last of the budget money yet?" I did not hear the Lance Corporal's answer because I had entered the staircase and was headed down already.

We past back through the room with the four desks to another room towards the runway end of the building. This was the workshop as the Gunny described the room we just entered to me. There at the end wall of the room was the large garage door that I saw from the outside a few minutes earlier. The room was eighteen feet wide, and at least double that in length which made it a big room. This I thought to myself was the cleanest workshop I had seen. The only thing out of place was a rusty absorber sitting in the middle of the room. There obviously was no work being done to repair this absorber, and from the looks of it none was planned. I asked the Gunny why the absorber was not in a container if no one was working on it. The Gunny explained that they were waiting for a Tech Rep to arrive from stateside. (A Technical Representative is an engineer from a civilian company to give advice about repair questions in the field.) He went on to talk about this special test they do for cracks. My mind clicked when I heard the words test for cracks. I spoke about the dye that you illuminate with a special light in the dark. I walked over to the workbench for a closer look at the tools available in this shop. I saw a box I knew should contain the tool we were talking about. I removed the toolbox from the shelf under the bench and set it on the floor. I opened the box showing the Gunny how this shop had everything it needed for the job. The words came out in my conversation that I performed this test at Futema and that the Marine Corps certified me to do this particular test. The Gunny kept asking me questions probing into the subject. The answers were coming out of my mouth but I was not sure I knew what I was talking about. I put the toolbox away and the Gunny and I exited the building for a tour of the out side around the MABS building.

We got into a gray pickup truck I had seen earlier and drove toward the runway. On the edge of the taxiway near the center point of the runway we stopped. The Gunny at that point spoke into a two-way radio. "5.0 request permission to cross runway". "5.0 clear" the radio responded. We crossed the runway approaching a sixteen by sixteen foot yellow shack located about fifty feet off the runway. There was no sign of life as the jeep stopped next to the shack door. Inside the shack the Gunny introduced me to a Corporal and five other Marines. These men were just laying around listening to a radio.

The Corporal and the Gunny took me for an inspection of the equipment used by this unit. We walked the fifty feet back to the edge of the runway, talking casually along the way. The absorber and retrieve engine sat in a pit on the edge of the runway in standby status. Everything was clean and shining with nothing out of place as if they were just show pieces. I asked the Gunny if the equipment was ever used. He stated last month or the month before they hooked an F-4 jet. After the three of us talked awhile longer the Gunny and I got back in the truck and headed to the shop.

The next morning I reported to the shop at 0800-hours as the Gunny ordered me the day before. I was ordered directly to the Captain's office. The Captain was impressed that I was certified to rebuild the absorber and had experience doing it. The absorber in the shop he described as an eye sore, degrading his unit. His profane description of Tech. Rep's and the length of time for them to respond showed an emotional side of the Captain. The Captain instructed me that any help or supplies I needed would be available. I was then ordered to work in the shop until my mission was completed.

The Lance Corporal from supply heard about the absorber being rebuilt. He immediately came to the shop area to talk with me about using as many supplies as I could. My explanation of repairing what I can did not sit well with the Lance Corporal. My being senior in rank limited what he could direct me to do. He left the shop area and I assumed the topic of new supplies had ended. The supply room had the Gunny issue an order that any non-major parts be replaced with new parts. I thought about what a waste of materials replacing parts would be, but at this point why not? Replacing the parts with new parts would get me to the runway crew faster. Leading a runway crew seemed like a dream come true. I had no idea what the job would consist of, but I would be a leader. How exciting! First I had to rebuild this absorber, so I had a mission to finish.

The first day I worked on dissembling every little piece of the absorber. By the end of the day shift, the parts were ready to be ground down to bare metal for inspection. I continued working; not realizing the chow hour had come and gone. The shop area seemed to be an area the men did not travel through, so it was easy to forget the time. The hour was 2330 when the runway crew stormed into the shop. They were unhappy because tower had kept them active on the runway. A fighter jet was due to land at some point that evening. The dirty condition of the shop sparked a few comments, about their day never ending. The crew leader asked how long before I finished, because it was their job to clean the building before they could go into the bunkroom. I told the Corporal I would assume responsibility for the shop area. Realizing at that point how late it was, I left for the barracks so the crew could sleep.

I was at the shop at 0500 the next morning working on the absorber. I had a mission, and I wanted to complete it successfully. At 0600 I rode with the runway crew to the mess hall for some Marine Corps chow. I pulled rank for my first time when I ordered the Marine in the passenger's seat into the back of the truck. The crew leader was sitting behind the steering wheel of the truck. This gave us a chance to become friends as we talked about what his job entailed. I picked up a few tips about how the shop is run on its daily routine. The Captain hates waves, as long as things go smooth and everything is kept clean the CO is happy. The crew leader asked me some questions during our conversation. He wanted to know what base I came from. I knew it was Okinawa, but my mind was a blank on any real facts about the island. I couldn't even remember the MABS unit number I was stationed at. My talk was so skimpy and evasive the Corporal started testing me as if I may be a liar. He knew a few men stationed on Futema so he asked questions about them. I had no memory on any subject and couldn't even explain why I didn't know. Of course, the crew leader thought that if I had just been there the answers should be readily available in my mind. The Corporal mentioned the name Steve, which rang a bell to me. A page in my mind must have opened at that point. I told the Corporal that Steve was my roommate. Then some of the things Steve and I did together started popping into my head. The corporal rationalized the other men he mentioned must have rotated before I got there. Breakfast ended and we were headed back to the shop on our daily routine.

I started each day at 0500 hours and worked until the runway crew came in at night. The Corporal from the runway crew placed in the logbook that a bag lunch was to be delivered to me by whom ever was driving "5.0" for the meal run. This helped because when I was working I would forget to eat. I was content with working in the shop and everyone seemed to like that and assisted me when ever possible. Everything continued on a positive track except for supply. The supply clerk worked at a slow pace. I found this out whenever I needed something from supply. My need for supplies could have been far less but I was under orders to use new parts. After awhile I became impatient with just waiting for the supply clerk to do his job. I started doing the paper work and retrieving the parts on my own. I worked long hours for seven straight days. The absorber was completed, into like new condition. The Unit Commanding Officer was happy the mission was completed. "Well done," he said.

I was assigned to be squad leader for a seven-man runway crew the day after I completed my mission in the shop. The first day started at 0600 hours when the runway crew reported to the shop for muster. The Corporal from the other crew handed me the logbook and the keys to "5.0". He quietly said good bye moments after he dismissed his men. I checked in the logbook for the departing crew's first entry two days earlier. I did as was done then. My role was identical to that of the leader before me. I called muster and cleared up a few orders, and then we went off to the mess hall. The men were friendly toward me at chow. I acknowledged their talk, but kept my distance. (NCO's cannot be friends with their men.)

The first week at the runway shack was pretty basic. We checked the gear for fluid levels and operational readiness first. This work would take thirty minutes or so to finish in what I assumed was the proper sequence. Once the work was completed the men would sit around the shack listening to music. At the 1200 hour (noontime) the crew would get into "5.0" for a chow run. After chow was consumed, it was back to the chairs in the shack listening to music. The clock strikes 1600 hours the crew gets back on "5.0" for another chow run. The most exciting part of the day was when I picked the tower phone up to ask if the runway was closed for the night. If the tower answer confirmed, we went back to the bunkroom to sleep. Our shifts were forty-eight hours on forty-eight hours off. The muster on the third day I handed the logbook and keys to the leader of that shift and went to my barracks. My social life was limited because of the amount of money I had for spending. Most of my time I spent writing letters, doing schoolwork, helping people, or exercising. My free time was very limited.

I continued the normal crew routine for three full shifts trying to learn the game. While sitting at the shack location I counted an average of forty-four fighter jets landing each day. The morning of the forth shift I called the tower and asked for a hook. That is a fighter jet dropping a tail hook from the rear of the plane and catching a wire rope across the runway. The process of the plane catching the wire rope and then the rope being rewound took eight minutes. During my time rebuilding absorbers in Okinawa the men bragged about time and how a short time means a better crew. This time kept flashing in my head as we again sat in the shack. The men in Okinawa bragged about how their time was seconds apart from catching one plane to being ready to catch the next plane. I thought about how that Marine grunts practiced their drills over and over to get they're timing faster. Why can't I drill my men to make their time faster? I thought.

I started a learning session of grouping the men and talking about the different jobs involved with a hook. Each Marine on the crew was required to talk about how to do one job. The discussions started with someone telling about point man. He had the longest distance to run but the least work. At point the Marine s job is to signal the pilot first if he caught the cable or not. If the hook skips over the cable the point man runs out on the runway and points the wands (flashlights with yellow cones) from his knee then extending his arms straight into the sky. He keeps repeating this until the plane is past him back into the air. If the hook catches the cable the point man signals the pilot that he hooked. This signal is to alert the pilot to release his throttle. In a matter of seconds the plane will stop its forward motion. The elastic tension in the nylon strap will pull the plane back wards twenty to thirty feet. When the tail hook clears the wire rope the point man signals to pick up hook and continue down the runway. The point man signals the engine operators to retrieve the rope at that point. The process all starts again for the next plane when the gear is ready. This should be completed--from hook to ready--in less than one minute.

The engine operator's job is first to make sure the gear is ready for the type plane on approach. The resistance indicator has to be set for the type plane on approach. The gear has to be free of all foreign obstructions for safety reasons. The retrieve engine has to be running before the ready signal can be given to the tower. After the plane lands he takes instructions from the point man until the plane clears the wire rope.

The boot runner is the person who places the blocks under the cable to raise it six inches. The elevation of the cable helps the hook catch it as the hook drags on the runway surface. His job sounds easy but when a plane catches the cable, the boots go flying in any direction. These boots can travel two to three hundred feet on each landing. The boot runner job falls on the engine operators when the crew is short handed.

The crew leader job is to keep in contact with the tower by phone or radio. He also has to see that every job is done properly and fill in where needed. This job is the where leadership is performed to enhance the efficiency of a crew. He can be needed in ten positions at once and he must see that each job is done. The need for split second decisions with heavy consequences must be made and enforced with no emotions. The crew leader is responsible for all the actions of the crew. Good or bad, this man can be hated and respected at the same time, but the success of the mission is all that counts.

I decided after the daily maintenance checks were done we would hold readiness drills. I told the men they had to run full speed to their positions each and every time. "Hurry up and wait" was a Marine saying that fit on this job. I would see every Marine run at full speed or they would all pay for that one Marine not following my orders. I drilled the men for the next three hours on running to their positions. I rotated the men to different positions and periodically questioned them on different jobs. I knew the theory of how the equipment worked but not the actual process of catching a plane. I had never seen a plane hook the gear that I knew of.

I called the tower six times for hooks on the second day of that shift. My way of concealing my ignorance was to do each job with a Marine looking over my shoulder. The men believed I was teaching them my way the process of doing each position works. I found out during the training session that some of the men had never caught a plane before either. The rest of the men at most had one or two hooks' experience themselves. They mostly remembered bits and pieces of what to do from what they learned in launch and recovery school. I learned the process from the men without anyone ever knowing I had never caught a plane before. My crew's hook time went from eight minutes to less than one minute in two weeks of training. We completed over one hundred practice hooks in that time. The men's mood appeared to be angry but I had no emotion when it came to job performance or the men. My men did their job and did it right every time, or else.

The logbook near the end of the second month at this base had an order written in it that I was to report to the Captain's office at 0900 hours. Why was I in trouble? What had I done this time was the only thought on my mind. I entered the Captain's office on time as ordered. The Captain placed me at ease standing in front of his desk. "Corporal Macdonald," the Captain said. "You have been here about two months." "Yes, sir" I responded. The Gunny, standing out of my line of sight stated, "I have requests from all seven men on your crew wanting to be transferred. What do you have to say?" I looked straight-ahead and responded in a Marine voice, "Gunny, these are my men and they will do the job until I am happy, unless I am ordered other wise." I was dismissed at that point. The whole event left me confused.

The next day while my crew was at the runway shack, the Captain and Gunny did a surprise inspection. At the time of the inspection I had the men doing their physical fitness training. The men, seeing the presence of the heavies, were thinking the exercise was over so they started looking happier. The thought that their leader would be busy at a meeting and not have the time to work them must have crossed their minds. I ordered the Lance Corporal who was next senior in rank to me, to run the men around the runway. The smiles on the men's faces disappeared. I salute the Captain and watched as the Gunny ordered four Marines out of the truck that had driven up behind the 5.0 truck. The television, radio, and all the furniture were removed from the shack. The tower phone and one wooden chair were left in what otherwise was and empty room. The crews were to exercise and work while at the runway shack. Those were the new orders given to each crew leader. This order was fine except after evening chow Armed Forces television comes on to entertain the men. This was the only English speaking television programming, and the men liked to watch it. The day is over at that point for the crew except for a possible emergency landing. The removal of furniture did not make sense to me. It seemed just to be a punishment for no reason.

The empty runway shack lasted for three of my crew's shifts. I thought during each of my shifts about a solution that would make everyone happy. The retired Marine said when he got my orders changed from Medical discharge to active duty. "Sometimes you just have to do things." The solution for me would be to just get some furniture to replace what was taken from the shack earlier. I didn't think the Captain nor Gunny would find out, after all the day they came was the first time I remembered ever seeing them at the shack. I put the Lance Corporal in charge of the runway crew with two other men under his command. I with the balance of my crew took "5.0" to the senior NCO's quarters located near the golf course on the other side of the base. I knew my men would never question my orders at any time. I marched them into the Senior NCO building giving the impression we were doing a job. A Master Sergeant at the TV room door was the only possible obstruction to completing my mission. I held some paper work in my hand and stated "Master Sergeant, I have a request to put a new television and furniture in this barracks. Is this the television room?" I asked, "This is the room Corporal. When will the new furniture be here?" the Master Sergeant wanted to know. "My men will remove the old furniture now and return with the new later today," I informed him. The Master Sergeant said "Very well." I ordered that my men load the truck with every item in the room. The runway shack now was equipped with a color TV plus clean comfortable furniture.

The tension on the base the next day could be felt every where. The senior NCO's wanted to know why supply did not deliver their new furniture on time. The supply unit wanted to know what happened to the old furniture. I did not anticipate the power a Master Sergeant had. He went to every unit on the base demanding someone come up with answers. The unit CO (the Captain) at 1830 hours muster assured us (our unit) had nothing to do with the incident. I believe that is also what he told the

Master Sergeant. The tension on base cooled down over the next few weeks. Everyone on the base was questioning where the furniture went but no one had the answer. The runway crews kept comfortable and quiet while fearing they could lose this furniture. At the next muster, I received orders to report to the unit office that day.

Chapter Twelve: Temporary assigned duty (TAD)

The Captain ordered that I was to report to flight line operations, after my shift was completed in the morning. I was to have a backpack with my shaving gear and a change of clothes in my possession at that time. The Captain then gave another order that to me seemed strange. Or maybe not, I told myself. Maybe this is normal procedure in the Marine Corps. I was ordered not to talk to anyone about reporting to the flight line operations building. At 0610 after my shift ended, I walked across the flight line to report as ordered. Just before reaching the building, a pilot ordered that I identify myself. I snapped a salute and followed the officer's orders. The officer then ordered that I was to board a small jet parked near by on the flight line. This trip seemed different. I kept repeating in my mind: is this the end for me? My mind formed the idea that my punishment for taking the furniture was death. The plane took off from the Iwakuni runway. For the next three hours I tried to close my eyes and sleep but my mind was too busy with questions. Interrupted by the wheels touching the runway, my mind was in a state of total confusion. I had lost track of what time in the day it was. My location was a mystery. The plane doors opened to a place I did not recognize. I had no idea if I had ever been here before. It sure was hot. The temperature must have been 120 degrees if not more. As quickly as I got off the plane I was boarded on to a CH-53 helicopter for another hour or so ride. The noise of the rotating blades of the chopper was nerve wracking as I just sat counting the times the blades past the window. It was late in the afternoon or early evening when we landed at another unknown base. The questions in my head had no answers. I was confused. My mind went on alert to defend myself in case this was the end of my life. Was this what happens for taking the NCO's furniture? Was I to be eliminated by the Captain's orders?

I got off the chopper in the mist of loud explosions off in a distance. A Navy Sea-bee went past me and I asked what the explosions were. He looked at me and smiled. In a loud voice to be heard above the noise he said "Don't use the outhouses at night. That is when they blow them up." A Marine with no shirt quickly escorted me away from the chopper. This Marine guided me to a Staff Sergeant working on an absorber in the pit on the side of the runway. I could only guess that I was at a MABS deployment unit, but why? There was so much happening around me. I just kept looking in every direction and ducking after each loud explosion. The Staff Sergeant grabbed me and jerked me into the pit. A cold angry look on his face, this Marine commanded, "Corporal your job is in the hole with me."

The Staff Sergeant explained how the absorber has a leak in the system and what they did to correct it. The rubber membrane in the tub had been changed. The leak still happened. They changed the rubber membrane twice more because they thought the rubber membranes were defective. The leaks still occurred. They then changed the entire absorber unit and the problem still existed. They next called Futema Marine Air Base in Okinawa to have a Tech Rep deployed. The clerk a Lance Corporal Steve advised him (the Staff Sergeant) the sixty-day time that it takes to get a rep sent from the world. I use the word world because that is what the military personnel refereed to the

United States. The clerk then advised him he knew someone just transferred to Japan that with a phone call he might get TAD (temporary assigned duty). The Staff Sergeant then informed me that I better be good because he wasn't pleased that they sent a Corporal. My mind was questioning if I was to be eliminated why are they asking about repairing gear. I looked at the absorber next to me. I couldn't remember how it came apart, never mind know how to fix it. My mind was a blank. Thoughts about Marines don't ask questions they do and die started racing through my head.

I helped the Staff Sergeant take the reel off the top of the absorber exposing the top flange assembly. We dissembled the main parts down to the rubber membrane located inside the tub. Parts of the repair job were flashing in my mind as we continued working. Remembering the names to the individual parts just did not happen for me. The Staff Sergeant's mood got angrier each time I referred to a part as the (what-cha-ma-call-it) or the (doohickey). His confidence in me was shrinking, but actually my understanding of the repair job was growing as I worked. I knew the problem when I saw the membrane and thought back to when we removed the reel a few minutes earlier. The work conditions and the method of removal damaged to the rubber membrane.

I showed the Staff Sergeant how to take three-foot sections of nylon strap off the reel at hand. That I was cutting sections off this Marine's equipment did not impress the Staff Sergeant. He commented that I better know what I am doing because I was destroying good Marine Corps equipment. I did not even think to ask about an old reel or something else that we could use. I just saw what I needed and took action. All six pieces of strap were placed over the edge of the absorber tub hole. The center section that the reel sits on was lowered into the absorber. The Staff Sergeant watched as the centerpiece rested on top of the six or so inches of the strap sticking out over where the centerpiece would go into. The centerpiece was lowered into the tub as it went down it pulled the straps into the tub with it a short distance. The straps prevented the centerpiece from hitting the rubber liner. This stopped any bruised or sliced spots to be left in the rubber after assembly. Just before the centerpiece was lowered the last inch or so the straps were pulled out. The tub settled right into its proper alignment.

The old liner that was removed from the absorber I picked up as I turned toward the Staff Sergeant. Mad as hell the Staff Sergeant was complaining how destroying a good reel was not necessary to do the job. Not realizing that it was me he was angry at, I showed him the damaged area in the rubber. As if I knew what I was talking about I went on with my explanation. In depth I explained about how pressure expanded the hole from the damage caused at installation. The change in pressure each time the absorber is used makes the unit useless in a short time. These thoughts about the repair job just kept coming to me as I spoke. My explanations were things I learned in Futema from other Marines when they taught me about repairing absorbers. Not accepting my explanation, the Staff Sergeant ordered me to "Get the hell off my base!" I started to explain that I didn't know where I was. The Staff Sergeant was so agitated that I just walked away. I had been wherever I was about five hours at this point. Questions were repeating themselves in my mind: (Where was I?)(Was I where I belonged?)

Walking around in the hot night air not knowing where to go just confused me more. Some men working under lights captured my eye. These were big lights shining on a work area so the men could work at night. The Marines under these lights were hooking up hydraulic lines to different parts of machines. Intrigued by the intensity of the men working I just stood and watched. One of the men turned his head and asked. "What do you need Corporal." I replied that I was just watching and asked. "What is all this?" The Marine stood up (he had no shirt on so I could not tell his rank) and said, "This is a two hundred and seventy two million dollar piece of junk." The conversation continued over a canteen of water being passed between us. The Marines explained how the system they were trying to assemble worked. The shirtless man was complaining about a tool that was needed for connecting a certain part was not transported with the unit.

There was a loud explosion of the side of the runway. One Marine chuckled and stated, "I hope no one was in that outhouse." I stood up and just looked around for a moment. Off a distance of a couple hundred yards I could see smoke rising. I turned back to the Marines in the pit and continued talking about the tool. It sounded to me as something pretty simple to make. I then made the comment, "Why not just make one?" Both Marines looked at me and said at the same time, "Yea, right." These Marines did not believe I knew what I was talking about. I actually did not know why I said that, but my imagination was thinking of solutions and I just went with it. The words from the other Marines started to be a series of comments or questionable remarks. A good example would be (what do we look like a department store or something?) At that point one of the Marines said "here is your chance use the out house that blew up and make our tool for us".

Those words to me sounded like a job. I had the Marine explain what they were trying to connect. They showed me this twenty-foot long tube. A special tool was used to guide this tension shaft down this tube. The tube itself was three or four feet diameter. Some one could walk down the tube when it was empty. The shaft that fit in took up a good part of that space in the tube. A bolt on the end of the shaft secured it to the tube. This shaft had to be guided down the tube at the proper elevation to align the bolt with the hole on the end of the tube. A large nut went on the out side of the tube so tension could be built up on the shaft. The tool then had to be removed without damage to any parts. My eyes were already searching for what was available. I had the thought in the back of my mind that survival is using what is around. I noticed to one side of the containers a stack of metal pipes or rods. They were twelve feet long and one inch by one-inch square metal tubes. I would need something a minimum of twenty feet in length. I had walked past a welder on the other side of the containers near the tool shed. I knew I could connect two rods end to end so that part of making a tool was done. Located under one of the fifty five-gallon oil drum was a dolly. I could take the wheels and axle off the dolly to make the rod mobile from one end. The next problem was how to hold the shaft on top of the tool at just the right height. I started walking around looking at everything for ideas. The amount of waste from the explosions was unreal. There were all kinds of objects to choose from, but the horseshoe shaped toilet seat caught my eye.

I took the measurements of the bolthole to the edge of the tube. I then measured the distance of the bolt from the edge of the shaft. I had to calculate the remaining space left over from the shaft when it was placed in the tube. The angle of the toilet seat mounted on the steel rod would be the way to solve the height for the bolt to enter the hole. I had forgotten about the correspondence courses. I had taken a course on math and did not remember until that moment. A geometry course was required if I wanted a high school diploma from Alton High School. I didn't understand how but as I thought about the angle of the toilet seat that triggered math equations in my mind. I started thinking how great a memory is for a Marine to do his job. I now was drawing thoughts from my brain that I had forgotten I knew. Learning and memory can be very important in life, I began thinking. My math was rough and I would be lucky if it works. However it appeared to others as though I knew what I was doing.

I was ready to build. I asked the two Marines if they would help. The mistrust or doubtful attitude of the others confused me but I had a mission. They helped by gathering the parts and following my directions on how to assemble the pieces. The first step was to weld the twelve-foot steel rod end to end. One Marine did that in a matter of seconds. The axle from the dolly was cut to a length of twelve inches. Welding the center of the axle to the steel tube with a wheel on each side had to be exact for it to work. A three-inch square flat metal piece was welded about two feet from the wheel end of the metal rod. This piece had to be at an angle so the toilet seat could be bolted to it. I calculated two feet from the end because that would allow one-inch movement in elevation from the other end of the steel rod when inside the tube. The closed end of the toilet seat was bolted to the metal plate through holes we drilled. The last thing was to remove some copper electrical wire from a wiring harness. I took small screws and connected each end of the three-foot wire to the open end of the horseshoe shaped toilet seat. I then connected the looped end of the copper wire to the steel rod. This wire I told the Marines was in case a piece of the toilet seat broke when we pulled it out. The broken pieces would come out with the assembly. The looks of the finished tool removed any mistrust remaining in the two Marine thoughts.

The true test of a tool was if it works. One of the Marines placed the shaft on top of the tool. As if custom designed, the horse shoe toilet seat cradled the shaft securely like a part stored on a supply shelf. The process of feeding the tool down the mouth of the tube was slow. We didn't want the toilet seat to break. Inch by inch, the belief that this tool would work grew. The assembly of this machine would allow the base to become functional as a part of the conflict around us. The true meaning of success came when the bolt lined up and come out the hole at the end of the shaft. After securing the shaft to the tube the tool was pulled back. The Marine pulling the tool noticed one side of the toilet seat had broken off completely. This was pulled out of the tube by the electrical wire. He commented how if the wire weren't there we would have to take the shaft out just to get the broken piece. The successful tool was left lying on the deck while we shook hands, congratulating each other.

The officer that was supervising the assembly noticed the tool where it was left after we finished. "Why did you bolt a toilet seat to the end of a steel rod?" he demanded to know. The officer went on to yell at the shirtless Marines. "We are in the zone! We have limited time and resources. We cannot afford to waste either!" I then spoke, "Sir, I am Corporal Macdonald. I take full responsibility." The officer stopped me from saying anything else. He wanted to inform me that charges would be filed, for misuse of government equipment, and willful destruction of government property. At that time a Major who was the chopper pilot who flew me in approached. He stated, "Corporal Macdonald, I am to take you out of here now." The junior officer looked at the Major and said, "What"? One of the shirtless Marines spoke up at that time, "I am a Gunny: Major. This Corporal designed and built a tool so we can get this base operational." The Major looked at the officer and said "Captain, the Corporal is going with me. Do you have a problem with that?" The Ch-53 took off in the dark before the sun could rise for the start of a new day. The next thing I remember was walking off of a plane landing at Iwakuni, Japan. I must have slept the entire trip back.

The first orders given to me when I entered the flight line operations building were to report to my MABS unit CO. The only possessions I had were in my backpack so I walked across the flight line to the MABS unit. I could tell the CO wasn't happy. I heard the CO's voice speak, "If that is Sergeant Macdonald, he had better get his ass at attention in front of my desk now." Some one must have told the CO that I was about to enter the building because of the timing of his order. I just opened the door to the building when his voice started echoing in the room. I responded as directed, because I was a Marine. The Captain rose to his feet placing both hands on the side of the desk as I entered his office. "I don't know how you do it Sergeant Macdonald." Even in a loud voice the CO words did not register in my head.

The words of the CO mystified me? What did I do wrong? I asked myself. I just answered, "Sir I do it for the Marine Corps." I thought the Captain was talking about the mission I was returning from. I thought maybe that the toilet seat disciplinary charges reached his desk already. The Captain's next words reinforced my thought of what I was in trouble over. The Captain asked the question, "Do you like making an ass out of me?" "No sir," I responded, "I was just helping Marines do their job better sir." The Captain then stated, "This whole base is being investigated to find who stole the TV room furniture out of the NCO's barracks. I personally denied any member of my unit had anything to do with it. The same missing furniture I personally found in the runway shack. My runway shack. I should place you in the brig. But I can't do that. I receive orders to promote you to Sergeant and transfer you to Thailand. Get out of my sight." I left the Captain's office not quite sure what reality was.

The Gunny met me on the other side of the Captain's office door. He handed me my Sergeant's promotion papers and a set of Sergeant's insignias for my work uniform. I followed the Gunny to the "5.0" truck, replacing my Corporal insignias with the Sergeant insignias as we walked. I was caught off guard. I did not want to ask a question and show I had no idea what had just happen. I just kept saying to myself "This is normal. I am experiencing something new. Play along." The Gunny dropped me off at the mess hall with the instructions to eat and then pack my gear. He would pick me up and transport to the flight line in time for my flight later that day.

I noticed a large box type truck was parked near the door to the mess hall. A Japanese man was struggling to get a box off the back of the truck by himself. I reached up on the truck and helped the man put the box on a dolly. This Japanese man seemed angry as he went on to explain why. He had planned to be home in thirty minutes for a family event, but a Marine ordered him to empty the truck before leaving. The boxes were too heavy for him to move he said. This will take all day. I put three boxes on his dolly and sent him off to transport the boxes inside. I climbed up on the truck and moved all twenty-seven remaining boxes up next to the rear door. The Japanese man was back as I jumped down off the truck. Quickly I put three more boxes on his dolly and off he went again. I happened to look across the street and noticed a four-wheel cargo dolly next to a parked truck. Without a second thought, I moved the dolly to the back of the truck that I was unloading. When the Japanese man came back the remaining twenty-four boxes were loaded on the cargo dolly. The Japanese man was all smiles as I steered the dolly with the Japanese man pushing into the building. Together we removed the boxes from the dolly into the mess hall supply room. The man kept shaking my hand and saying, "Thank you." I kept saying, "No problem" back to him. I believe the man told me his name was Mr. Hoo but every time I called him that, he would say Hoo back. I finally broke away from Mr. Hoo and went in the mess hall to eat.

The "5.0" truck arrived at the barracks that afternoon. I put my gear in the back of the truck and then climbed in the cab. The Gunny started talking the moment the truck door closed. "Sergeant, you make one hell of a good Marine." He went on talking about my wiliness to put my career on the line for my men's comfort. The Gunny said he thought I was a fool until I stood my ground with the Captain. He went on to tell me how the Captain went out to the runway shack to talk with the men in the unit. He wanted to know why every man wanted to be transferred off my crew. He then made every man of the unit below Corporal answer questions anonymously. The survey showed the men were pissed because you work, train and make them do physical fitness classes. The Gunny went on to say your crew's performance statistics are the best in the Marine Air Wing. The most surprising point that over whelmed the Captain was that not one man wanted to be on my runway crew here at Iwakuni. But when asked about if they were in a combat situation, every single Marine picked me as their platoon leader. The "5.0" truck approached the stairs leading up to the plane, then stopped. The Gunny shook my hand and stated, "Sergeant Macdonald, I don't think the Marine Corps is ready for you. I get out in thirty days so I will not have the privilege of having you in my unit again. Good luck". I got on the plane with my gear. I was off to Thailand.

Chapter Thirteen: Pain

I landed in Ubon, Thailand on a bright, sunny, hot day. The easy life that I had enjoyed as a Marine was now over. I was a Marine located in what is referred to as a "non-combat zone during a conflict." The administration system seemed different on this base than at any other place I had been stationed at so far. The first place that a "new be" checks in is at the unit office. On other bases the command tells you the unit after completing the base check in. In Thailand the American Marine unit is attached to the Thailand Air Force as a deployed support unit. The American unit command has total control of a Marine attached to it. I was given my barracks assignment, which sounded pretty impressive at the time. A Sergeant got one half of a building as his place to call home. Impressed with the idea of living on this base, my first day was mine to settle in and learn the base layout. I carried my duffel bag down a dirt path between wood screen, metal roof shacks called hooches.

The private I was walking down the path with pointed to a side path as he talked about the base. I looked down the deeply worn red clay path to a series of four-foot square shacks. "There is the bathroom," the private said with a chuckle. We walked another fifty feet or so. That is when the private pointed toward a path on the opposite side. A metal roof building with walls, that looked like two-foot wide towels wrapped around it came into view. You could see into the room above the walls and below the walls. I noticed the showerheads were hanging from the ceiling. "There is the shower," the private said. Then the private added a warning, "The hot water only last for the first shower each day." I asked, "Why?" So the private explained that the only heating system is the sun, and when the water in the pipes is used up-- that's it. The private then surprised me when he said, "we're here." The private stopped at a "hooch" in the area with identical hooch's on both sides of the path. These hooches were in the middle of rows of hooches that looked identical. I asked, "Is this my building?" The private agreed, saying "Welcome home."

Each hooch had a floor size of twelve feet by twenty feet. A door was located at opposite ends of the building. This made a private entrance for each sergeant, because inside a wall divided the hooch in half. The outside walls were solid up two feet from the floor. There was a screen from the top of the wall to the edge of the roofline. A series of ten-inch wide boards nailed at forty-five degree angels to the outside of the screens provided privacy. Inside there were three wall lockers, a cot, small table and one chair. The private then pulled out a net and said, "This is for the bugs." And he warned me to lock everything up at night, because the Thai people would steal what is not locked. This made me wonder about base security.

I unpacked my gear, which didn't take me long. I decided a walk around the base would give me a chance to see where I was relative to the base layout. I walked a distance trying to remember how to get back to my hooch. A problem materialized before I got far. I became confused. By this time in my memory-shortened life, I had started to realize that my mind was forgetful. Just then two Marines said, "Hey you look like a new be." I stopped and talked to these men in the hope of learning my location on the base. I sat for a time enjoying a beer that one Marine handed me. The conversation lasted awhile and then I started back in the direction I came from. Enjoying meeting new people and the friendship that was born, I forgot to ask my location. I took a path to the left, then the right, with the desire to solve the problem on my own. I dreaded the thought of going back to ask directions. I kept saying to myself that everything looks the same. But I can solve the problem. I had no idea where my hooch was located. Everything looked the same. I stood in one spot looking, trying to identify which hooch was mine. I heard a plane take off in the area just behind a row of hooches. I now had a reference point. I headed toward the runway. My unit was always located on the flight line, and I knew this. My plan was to seek help locating the position of my hooch from the men in my new unit.

I got to the MABS unit just as the eighteen hundred-hour chow run was loading on a truck. I rode to the mess hall with the runway crew. The location of the mess hall was something that I needed to know. I ate chow with the Sergeant in charge of the runway crew on duty. We had an interesting conversation, asking questions back and forth. I was asking questions of him about how I would work into the flow of this unit. We ate some of the worst food in the dirtiest conditions I have seen. The other Marines were either conditioned to eat it or unaware that it was bad food. Being hungry helped me stomach the food but I ate only enough to satisfy my body's need. After chow, the Sergeant drove to a path that led to the village of hooches. After walking a short distance he showed me which hooch was mine. At the time I got out of the truck, my hand grabbed a can of yellow spray paint from the truck floor. On the way down the path, I painted a small dot on several hooches in the empty space above each door. This way, I would not loose my hooch again.

The Sergeant gave me some advice as we walked to my hooch as a follow up to my earlier talk at the mess hall. "The conditions are relaxed here. Do your job and let the men do their job." He went on to say, "If mistakes are made, whitewash it. We are short handed and low on supplies. After everything cools down, show the proper way you want the job done." I went into my hooch and lay on the cot to think about everything that was happening to me. Was living here in Thailand real? My mind was caught between the fading memory of living conditions on the last base and the poor conditions here.

The rain beat constantly on the metal roof of my hooch the entire first night. I was still awake at 0430 hours the next morning, so I decided to get the hot water. I put on my shower flip-flops and stepped out of the hooch. My feet sank in the clay and my flip-flops stayed in the spot I had first stepped. I reached down into the mud with my hand to pick out the flip-flop from below the surface. The mud stuck to my hand as I pulled the flip-flop out from the mud. I finally reached the shower only to find that although the water was not cold it was only slightly warm. My mind started accepting these conditions as normal conditions in real life. I stood on the two-foot square rubber mat and washed the mud off my body. I finished my first shower in Thailand still questioning myself as to my existence in life. Heading back to the hooch, my mind accepted Thailand as the conditions everyone in the world lived. My car accident after boot camp had left my memory limited to only remembering recent events. My memory varied. Sometimes I could remember events for days, weeks, or months. Other events, I forgot seconds after they occurred. When I did arrive back at my hooch, I looked down at my feet and legs to find them covered with red clay.

My next stop was to report to the MABS unit for my new assignment at 0730-hours that morning. I arrived at the unit and was assigned to the position as the new shop NCO. I would be working alone at the job of keeping the runway gear in operation. I walked over to the area pointed out as my shop by the administrative Marine. The shop building was made of empty metal containers stacked in rows to resemble walls. A makeshift roof was placed on top, giving the appearance of a building. The tools were limited. To make a supply room, they took empty container eight feet wide and twelve feet long, with one eight foot high wall removed for the entrance. The supplies were very limited, very little was on the makeshift shelves. I had been told there was no functional back-up gear for the runway. The gear in use on the runway was in need of repair. This gear on the runway was used every day and broke down regularly. This unit worked hard at their job of launch and recovery of aircraft for long hours each day and night. The unit put off the maintenance because of the lack of manpower, knowledge of the process, and supplies to do the job.

There were three absorbers in various stages of disassembly, just lying around my work area. I spent the next day assessing the damage to each tub. Anyone else probably would have started repair work immediately with his knowledge of the work involved. The problem was that I had to remember what was involved with doing whatever it was I was suppose to do. A tub is the base unit to an absorber. Observing the different damaged parts, made my memory click. The job was major and the supply container seemed useless to provide what was needed to do the job. I went in the office to discuss the options of getting what I needed for supplies. The First Sergeant said the strangest thing at this time, "You were transferred here because you can fix anything with what ever supplies you have. Get to work, Sergeant." I left the office trying to understand what was happening. I got back to the shop area and all I could remember was the phrase: "Survival is using what is around you." I just started looking around the area. I had a mission now.

The first step in my new job would be to disassemble the three absorbers completely. In my mind, I rationalized the question of how hard can taking something apart be? I set up a staging area so as the parts came off I could lay them out for viewing. I also wanted to keep the parts in the order they came out, so I could put them back. The absorber is a five-foot by seven-foot tub made of steel. The tub holds water, which is directed through different guides, which spin in the middle assembly. A reel of nylon tape (one half inch thick by six inches wide) seats on top of the middle assembly. The nylon tape is one thousand feet long, spun around the reel so one end hangs off. The tape is pulled to the side of the runway and connected to one side of the deck pennant. This is the wire rope the plane hook catches when landing. To start the job I needed specific tools. I looked for the pull tool used to remove the rollers from the absorber post. My mission became difficult because the tools were limited to a few basic general shop items. My mind worked in strange ways. Information to do a repair job just came to me. I had no idea where I found this information. My mind was like opening a book of directions. The pages in my mind seemed to turn, as I needed to know things.

To remove the rollers, I would need to lift them evenly off the post. I looked around as my imagination started working. The first need was claws (something to act as fingers under the bottom edge of the rollers) that were strong but wouldn't damage the smooth surface of the roller. I looked at the skids under the metal containers used as the walls of my shop. These were attached I-beam units that worked like skis attached to the containers. I cut a couple of two-inch wide sections of the I-beam off a container that was not in use. The top outer edge of the "I" was removed so it looked like an upside down L on a line. On the upside down L near the intersection (or vertex), I drilled a hole and bolted a chain. The other end of the chain was connected to a metal bar two feet long one half inch thick and three inches wide. This top connecting bar ran across the top of the rollers. The other chain and claw was attached in the same manner as the first chain and claw. This was connected on the opposite end of the connecting bar running across the top of the roller. In the middle of the top connecting bar I cut a hole. I put a one-foot long bolt two inches thick through the hole. I put the nut on the bolt that ran through the hole and started screwing it in until the claws tightened under the bottom edge of the roller. The tip of the bolt went on the center of the roller post as the roller assembly lifted off. I did this process on the three absorbers I was working on. Once all six rollers were removed from the three absorbers, I went to the next step. The challenge of solving problems motivated me to get the mission done.

I removed the flange (center assembly) on which the reel sits. The flanges were the parts I would grind down and check for cracks. A complete check could not be done, so I just inspected each flange closely with my eye. There was no way the naked eye could spot a crack, but I did not understand that at the time. These inspections were done during the time when the parts came off the absorber being disassembled. I disassembled all three absorbers down to single parts. The larger parts were power washed and wiped down dry. The smaller parts I washed and wired brushed in a wash tub made out of half of a fifty-five gallon drum. The absorbers were ready to be reassembled at this point.

The assembly of the absorbers was a contest in itself to me. I started with the flanges, which sit inside a heavy rubber liner. These liners stretch to a degree allowing the assembly to build water pressure as the plane pulls out the tape. The pressure increases the vortex action (water directed in different directions causing a braking resistance) as the reel spins. The rubber liner allows the absorber to adjust itself at different speeds as the reel is turned. I had only one new liner to work with. I had three old liners with different number of holes in each one. The best of the damaged liners was solid on the sides but a pinhole in the bottom made it useless. I took the best of the old liners and cut the bottom out of it. I coated the bottom inside of a different old liner with rubber glue, then placed the cut bottom on top of the glue. The rubber glue I borrowed from another unit's supply truck that was unoccupied on the flight line. This solution worked in my mind, and the thought of it breaking while in use on the runway never entered my mind.

The rollers were the next step to put together and install. There were retainers, spacers, sleeves, and many other parts to rebuild this assembly. To be right, these parts should have been replaced with new parts. I did not have most if any of this assembly in supply. The slow cleaning process of soaking the parts in gas began. I lightly rubbed the parts with steel wool pads in an attempt to save most of them. Any parts saved and not used were put in the supply container. The final part of rebuilding the absorber is the tension arm and tension roller.

The absorber on the front runway side has a tension arm. This tension arm is mounted opposite the rollers. The purpose of the arm is to keep the nylon strap tight when being pulled out or reeled in. This assembly went together easily until I got to the retainer snap ring at the end of the roller post. This ring looks like a horseshoe, where the open end is bent closer together. They are expanded over the post and then let free. They act as a metal elastic ban and snap back. The ring fits into a groove in the post to stop the arm from coming off the post. I had no snap rings. The need to check the area for whatever was available got me to walking around the unit. The First Sergeant had his shirt hanging on a metal coat hanger, I remembered this as I past the office door.

I went into the office and took the coat hanger off the wall and headed back to my shop. I bent the wire to the shape of the snap ring. I then took the new ring and filed the top and bottom sides flat, so when placed around the post they fit snug into the cut grove in the post. I had left the coat hanger wire long so at the open part of the snap ring I could bend the wire out so the excess wire stuck away from the post. I used some eighteen-gauge wire to tie the coat hanger ends of my snap ring together. The last thing I did was to bend the excess coat hanger wire away from the safety wire to lock it in place. The excess coat hanger wire was cut off to make it look good. I was finished. The two rebuilt absorbers were ready to be pressure tested.

The shortest day I worked since starting these repairs was seventeen hours. Things in Thailand were different in the working and living conditions. I was a Marine beginning to believe this way of living was the way life was for everyone in the world. We did not have to muster each day. There were no inspections. Everyone knew what his or her job was and did it. I had set up a cot in an empty container and when I was tired, I slept. The food was bad, but when I was hungry I would go to the mess tent and enjoy what I could get. I liked to keep busy because the other choice was to do nothing but lay around the hooch thinking. The other men would talk about their past and things that they remembered. I enjoyed talking and meeting everyone I could, but I never had much to say. I had only a short memory of my past, which limited my contribution in any conversation. I could not remember the specifics on events that happened after the accident back in New Hampshire. I knew the countries and bases I had been on but I could not remember any other parts about my stays at these places. The conversation I would have always seemed to start the other men questioning my honesty about my life. I found that even in Thailand, having no memory fascinated others. The idea someone could not know about their past was difficult for others to accept. They could never believe it possible so my honesty would be in question. My mission at the shop was done so I had the day off in my hooch to get things done that I had been putting off.

I was writing a letter when the base went on full alert. I could hear the planes scrambling to take off from the runway, one after another. The paths were filled with Marines trying to get to their jobs. I was lying in my cot trying to talk in a letter to someone I did not remember. My mother wrote me at least once a week, but I knew her as the lady who visited me at Portsmouth Naval Hospital. I had a vague memory of the Navy hospital but I hardly remembered if I had been there or not. My letters from my mother described things that I had no idea about. My family, home, the town of Alton, I knew about these people and places from what she told me. The reinforcement of her weekly letters allowed me to remember what she was telling me but not retain complete stories. There was a lot in my past I had no knowledge of because no one ever spoke of it. A knock on the door was a PFC telling me I was needed at my unit. I scrambled to join the other men on the paths, all in a mad rush in a direction toward the runway.

I was told at the shop that one of the retrieve engines on the active gear was making a clinging noise. I got to the site in time to watch the connecting rod explode out the side of the diesel engine. The Corporal in charge of the crew was down and out as the rod bounced off the side of his head. I helped another Marine place the Corporal in the back of a parked jeep. I ordered one of the two men to take the Corporal to the medical unit and return to the runway as soon a possible. The other crewmember I ordered to go to the unit shop. I told him that a retrieve engine was to be loaded on a truck and brought to the runway. I looked around the area for the rest of the crew. Normally a seven-man crew is used for manning the gear. Here in Thailand they were short of men, so three men made a crew. I jumped in the absorber pit (a hole in the ground so the reel is level with the runway surface) and started disconnecting the retrieve engine. A retrieve engine was needed to retract the nylon strap after a plane hooked. You could take one hook without the retrieve engine to retract the deck pennant.

The new engine was bought out with a forklift with in a matter of minutes. The crew member couldn't find a forklift operator. This Marine took the first forklift he saw and drove it himself. The forklift with an engine hanging from a chain drove up next to the pit. He set the engine down on the flight line. We then connected the engine in the pit with a chain to be picked up and taken out of the pit. The chain was looped over the fork and hooked on the lifting plate of the engine. The fork lift operator picked the engine straight up and started to back away. The forklift jumped and the chain slide off the fork letting the engine fall. I did not think of the consequences when I pushed the engine away from the pit. The crewmember that drove to sick bay had returned and was in the pit, bent over. This engine, if allowed to fall, would have hit the Marine bent over in the pit. The engine with me pushing cleared the edge of the pit and smashed on the flight line. I landed in the pit beside the absorber. I had sharp pain in my lower back as my eyes opened looking at the floor of a greasy pit. I knew the mission was to get the retrieve engine installed and the gear on line.

I was lying flat in the pit and every time I moved the pain got worse. My legs were numb and tingling. The pain was causing my body to twitch. The two-crew members out side the pit came running to help me. I thought about my feelings and emotions being stored in a paper bag. I had a mission that must be completed. I separated the pain from my body and started sizing up what needed to be done.

The men tried to help me up, but when I bent the pain got worse. The thing that caught my eye was a bundle of runway matting locking bars. (These are eighteen-inch long one half inch wide made of quarter inch thick aluminum sticks used to hold the portable runway together). I had one of the men lay two three foot long pieces of duct tape on the deck sticky side up. Both the men placed the locking bars on the tape four inches apart. They took two more three-foot pieces of duct tape and put it on top of the locking bars sticky side down. The men then picked me up from the deck. One man held me up. The other man wrapped the locking bar assembly around my waist and duct taped it to me. Nice and tight to hold me stiff, because when I moved, it hurt.

The problem was we were still on alert. The planes were due back in a few hours from their missions. The cycle of planes to take off and land was only beginning. The men leaned me against something and I instructed the men on how to install the engine. The men, pretty much knew what to do on their own. I just filled in a few directions when needed. We finished the job with only minutes before the first hook arrived.

A normal crew consists of seven to ten men. A three-man crew meant a lot of work for two men. The point man only had to direct planes because he was eight hundred feet up the runway. His primary job when the plane hooks is to direct the pilot to unhook. His secondary job is, if the hook does not catch the wire rope to signal the pilot to take off again. The two retrieve engine operators would have to place the boots. (Half of a car tire used to hold the deck pennant up off the runway). They would also have to operate the tower phone and retract the nylon straps. I did the phone and one engine while the other crew member chased the boots, and retracted his gear. The next twenty-four hours were long. I wished that so many times that night I would die.

The alert ended around 0730 in the morning. The two-crew members during the night, while the offensive was happening, duct taped a pole that reached from the ground to above my head to my back. I was then duct taped to the engine housing so I would not fall over during the alert. After the alert ended, I was cut free from the pole then placed in a jeep to be transported to sick bay. The problem was I could not sit or lay down in the jeep. I stood in the passenger side holding onto the windshield. I was taken directly to the medical unit.

The Navy corpsman just shook his head when he saw me duct taped while standing in a jeep. This man's opinion of Marines was not that high. The dude was a Navy medical aid not even a corpsman. Someone in civilian life would call him a male nurse's aid. He cut the duct tape away from my uniform. He then removed the locking bars. He kept poking my lower back to cause pain as if he enjoyed it. He finally stood me up and wrapped two ace bandages around my waist, one on top of the other. I received one-week light duty for a diagnosis of a pulled ligament and ordered back to my unit.

I was in a lot of pain for the next week. I could not stand for a very long periods of time. I could not sit or lay for long periods at any one time. I was restless, bored and out of control trying to get answers from the medical aid station. The Navy guy kept telling me, "You are a Marine. You can take the pain." I believed what this medical expert was telling me. The longer into the week it went the more I could do by enduring the pain. I went back to work on the eight day because I could not stand being idle.

I could not bend over, pick anything up, or walk fast. Other than that I was fine. The pain was still controlling what I could do. The work I could do was held to a very limited number of things. The leaders in my unit were now starting to question my usefulness to the unit. The rumors starting to circulate about my transfer could be heard around the unit.

Chapter Fourteen: Duty

The Base commander for American forces sent a memo to each American unit looking for a volunteer to ride in a convoy at a NCO pay grade. Ubonn was a Royal Thai Air Force Base that we shared with Thai forces. The American forces stationed at this base were guests on temporary assignment. My shop CO, aware of my medical situation, volunteered me for this assignment thinking that my riding in a truck would be light duty. The shop CO explained how I would get to see the countryside of Thailand and enjoy the easy life. I was excited about the convoy because sitting around in my hooch all the time made my mind want to think too much. I would daydream every idle moment about what it must be like back in the world (United States) from things I had heard. Other Marines would tell stories about their experiences back in the world. People speaking English, flush toilets, the stories all seemed unreal to me lying there on a base in Thailand with back pain. What was I waiting for? Is this what life is all about? Is life back in the world like it is here?

My memory of ever living any place but here in Thailand had faded. I had the letters I received from my mother and girl friends telling me about life back in the world. I had to ask myself, Were these people real? Thinking while by myself was a problem for me. I had no avenue to relate what I was thinking to a memory to indicate if I had done the event that I was thinking about. It was like talking about Okinawa, Japan, or El Toro. I knew I was stationed at these places. The reality was I could not describe a single fact about any place or thing before I entered Thailand. I had no memory except of my surroundings that existed now. I would do things and have a flash memory of the mechanics, but no thoughts of people involved or décor of the area when the flash memory occurred. I accepted this as the way things were for me. I was happy with the idea of being able to remember how to work. Why could I remember how to work and not other things? Why did I remember that I could not remember? The Base CO's need for volunteers was a needed remedy to my "thinking problem."

I received orders to get my M-16 rifle out of the attack locker. Attack defense boxes were staged around the area to control the misuse of weapons. One of the reality of war is everyone has a weapon in their possession. It was believed some of the men when they got mad would shoot to eliminate the person they were mad at. All the military investigation came up with was American ammo was being used to shoot too many officers. Hence they solved the problem with the staged ammo lockers. I was issued two magazines of twenty rounds each, a pouch for the magazines, an ammo belt, and canteen for the trip, along with my rifle. A Staff Sergeant at the departure point handed a detailed description of what my job and responsibilities were to me. My position for the ride would be in the lead truck of a convoy of Thai trucks carrying American military equipment. My job was to protect the paper work (inventory of the cargo) with my life. The weapons in my possession were not to be lock and load; that is, they were not to be ready to fire at a moment's notice. The orders clearly stated that before lock and loading a weapon the Marine must be in eminent danger of death. The Marine Corps did not care about cargo on the trucks, which didn't make sense. The paper work was to never leave my sight. That was my only responsibility. I had many possible questions. But Marines never question, just do and die.

In my daily routine, if I noticed someone needing help, it was common for me to give that person a hand. I had over the months in Thailand helped many people with different things, never wanting anything in return. The Staff Sergeant introduced me to the lead truck driver at the staging area. I recognized his face but didn't know his name because we never talked when we were together or I just did not remember. On several occasions this driver was loading his truck, as I would be passing by. To help someone for a few minutes makes this world a better place to live, I believed. After the loading was complete, I would just leave with a handshake and a thank you. When he noticed me, this driver was happy as he shook my hand with a smile. He started speaking broken English telling the Staff Sergeant how I helped him load heavy boxes on his truck.

This man's truck could have come from the nineteen thirties. I believe this same type truck I had seen in a gangster movie about some person in Chicago. I had seen this movie in the recreation tent. The truck had the running board fender over the front wheels, with the 1930 model hood. This truck had a straight flat windshield with little windshield wipers hanging from the top. There were no doors, just a bench seat that extended a foot out the side of the cab. Comfort did not enter my mind when I saw the back of the seat was the metal cab structure it self. The back area of the truck was a flatbed. It extended at least twenty feet past the dual rear wheels. The load this man had on his truck far exceeded the weight capacity recommended for any vehicle. My daily routine in my hooch needed change at this point. I would have taken any job that anyone offered. I set aside any reasons for not going on this assignment, not that I had a choice.

The Convey departed the base at 0800 hours the next morning. I had my shaving gear, a change of clothes, my rifle and not much more. The paper work for the adventure was my main concern and I held the papers tight in my hands. The road that we traveled on in the beginning was a bumpy dirt road. The overloaded truck made the ride even rougher than it should have been. We weren't but five kilometers down the road when my back pain got worse than it had ever been. I tried sitting on my hands as a remedy. When that did not work I placed my hands on the ceiling of the truck to keep from bouncing, but nothing worked. The pain by the time we stopped for lunch was causing water to form at the edge of my eyes. My friend the driver kept asking me, "Are you all right?" I had explained the back problem to him when we were driving earlier. He was aware of my condition. After the first time the driver asked, my signal to the driver was a thumbs up signal to tell him I was OK. The ride continued for a couple more hours, then all the trucks stopped at an intersection.

My driver signaled sixteen trucks to continue down the road on their own. Our truck and four others turned a corner onto a different road. The driver told me this was the way to his village, where we would spend the night. The road would steadily go up hill, then level off for awhile, then start up again. People were working the farmland all over the place as we passed through the countryside. Old men and women, children each with their hands or basic homemade tools would be working in the fields and rice paddies. The temperature must have been one hundred and twenty degrees, yet these people were working hard and continuously. I on the other hand was working hard to accept the pain, hoping someone would shoot me. The day had been long as I counted the minutes and hours we had been driving. Nighttime had arrived as the five trucks pulled into a village. A woman squatting on the side of the road taking a pee marked the spot where the truck started to slow to a stop. We parked only feet past this squatting woman by front door of a straw thatched hooch.

Getting out of the truck was trouble for me. The pain in my back and numbness in my legs made it hard to move or walk. The five drivers and I proceeded into the hooch. Once inside, the driver introduced me to an old lady as his mother. My guess was her age was about forty-five years old not much more. The girl next to him looked about twelve years old. The driver said, "This is my wife." At that point the five drivers plus myself were in a circle on the floor around a cloth table. The two women severed us all rice and green leafy cooked vegetable meal, on what looked like a board. We ate with our fingers. It was simple as meals go, but the taste was better than Marine rations I was issued for the trip. The meal ended as the women brought a bottle of after dinner drink to the men. At that point the women removed the food boards from the table as if they were servants in a peasant society.

The men started passing the bottle from one man to the next. Each man would take a drink, make a face, and hand the bottle off to the next man. I was handed the bottle by it being place on the floor in front of me. I put the bottle to my lips and took a big drink of some really rot gut alcohol type beverage. I liked it. The warmth of it going down made the pain in my back ease some. I lowered the bottle from my lips to pass it to the next in line. I extended my arm holding the bottle out in front toward this man. The pain was crippling, causing my body to move uncontrollably. I jack knifed my body in a pain with a wrenching motion on the floor. I held my butt high off the floor grabbing my back with one hand. The men started talking to each other with excitement. They were amazed that I was in such pain but held the bottle in my other hand without spilling it. The driver at that point said something to the women as they walked over to me.

The next man in line took the bottle out of my hand, which helped reduce some of the pain. I felt the two women slowly helping me up from the floor. They walked me about five feet to the corner on the other side of the room. There was a blanket spread on the floor like it was their bedroom area. The women one at a time let go of me. The woman not holding me took off her clothes then traded places while the other undressed. I had trouble accepting that two naked women were now undressing me. I looked at my driver, who was the young woman's husband. There must have been words written on my face at that moment. The driver responded to me, "They will be privileged to massage you. They don't want to get the salve on their clothes." I was now lying on the blanket feeling these women rub this slimy goo on my back. I fell into a deep sleep as these women eased my pain.

The next morning, the pain in my back was minor until I started to get up from the floor. I looked beside me to see if the paper work was still with me. Then I realized that I was standing naked in a stranger's house. Neatly folded and piled at the edge of the wall were my clothes and next to them, my M-16 rifle. I slowly got up and put my pants on when the wife and driver came into the room. The driver was speaking the Thai language to his wife as they entered. She took one of the boards used the night before as a plate and before I could buckle my pants placed it against my lower back. She slowly wrapped the ace bandages (that were removed the night before) around me nice and tight. The driver still was talking the whole time as if giving her directions in their own language. The board limited my motion but I could at least walk.

The events of this day pretty much set out the same as the day before. We drove hour after hour. The ride was uncomfortable and painful as the day before. The board helped me keep my back straight keeping the ride from causing the pain to get worse. The heat from the sun got intense about midafternoon. I could feel the water dribbling down my back off the board causing my butt to get wet. The smell of my body from sweat and the salve plus dirt was obnoxious. The truck driver laughed and said, "You stink." I agreed with him, but for the next couple of hours there was nothing I could do.

The trucks pulled into a village with a large number of men in robes walking around. It was dark by this time as we entered the village area. I noticed some water running off a rock just off the side of the road. The water would fall about four feet into a small puddle on the ground and run off to one side of the road into a ditch. The driver (my friend) told me one of the other drivers lived here in this village and his family would feed us tonight. I acknowledged what he said as the truck stopped. I got out and then reached back in the truck and got my backpack, along with my other gear and the paper work, leaving the belt with the ammo. The other five Thai men had gone in to the house by this time without me. I had signaled them that I would be right behind them as they left. I at that moment decided to walk back up the street to where I had seen the water to check it out. I looked around and noticed there was no one else in the area of the water at this time. I took my clothes off and got the soap out of my bag. I sat in the puddle as if it was my private bathtub. I washed my body several times with soap and water until I felt clean. I brushed my teeth put clean clothes on and packed everything including the paper work in my backpack. I noticed six monks at this time (men in robes) watching me. I started to walk back to the truck but they swarmed around me. One of the monks spoke English pretty clearly. I was ordered by this English speaking Monk to go with them. They seemed nice and the English-speaking monk explained to me why I needed to go with them. I needed to have God clean my soul at their temple because I just washed in their holy faucet. According to the Monk the holy place was only up the road a short distance and I could come back after the blessing was over. I decided fighting was not needed. I went with them willingly. We got up the road a bit out side the village and I saw a campfire glowing in the bushes. The distance we traveled wasn't far, I thought, as we neared the glow of the fire. Three men (not from Thailand) with rifles took my M-16 and backpack from me as we approached. They told me to sit down in a spot near the fire. I knew I was in trouble by this time but I remembered (from where I don't know) "Good Marines don't come back alive." This thought made me have the desire to learn more about what was happening to me. I was sitting by the campfire with the others and all I could think was I have been here before. I fell asleep feeling kind of safe, but having one hand tied to one of my feet wasn't that comfortable. I assumed this was the blessing process but felt at the same time maybe it wasn't. Having one hand tied to my foot made me question the event.

The time was late at night because it was dark and the moon was beginning to set. I had fallen asleep next to the fire. I felt a hand shake my shoulder. The fire had burned down to hot ashes as I saw there were only two men with rifles sleeping near by. My friend held one finger to his lips as he untied the rope from my ankle with his other hand. I got up slowly as my driver friend helped me move away from the area. I picked up my backpack from next to a rock as we left. My M-16 rifle was not in the area but at that point I could not have cared less about it. No rifle would mean less weight I thought as I tried to ignore the pain in my back.

We had walked about fifty feet when the driver pulled my shoulder down in a hushing motion. On one knee I could hear the missing man talking to himself patting the side of the M-16. The man walked within six inches of us but he was so happy patting the side of the M-16 he didn't notice us. He had just passed by us when he realized we were hiding in the dark. I put my left hand over his mouth and pulled his knife out from the holster holding it to his side. The entire process of what the Marine Corps trained me for, it all became apparent to me in a flash. My mind became one with the idea of completing the mission with no obstacles preventing me from doing that job. It was the fastest second ever as the knife went up under his rib cage, at a forty-five degree angle. I twisted the knife back and forth following the example that the flashes in my head were demonstrating. I held the man up with my thumb on one of his cheeks and fingers on the other squeezing his mouth as a vice clamps an item. I lowered him to the ground with the hand holding his face as his motions stopped. I grabbed my M-16 with one hand and followed the driver back to the truck still parked in front of the hooch.

The driver went in the hooch to get the other men. I reached in to the truck for my belt that had the ammo magazines on it. I went to lock and load when I noticed the man had his own clip in my weapon. The blood on my hand and rifle now stood out as I looked at them. I walked over to the water where this evening all started and washed the blood off my rifle and me. The drivers were all starting their trucks as I got back from the water. We were heading down the road within minutes of my return.

It must have been close to morning by this time. The sun was clearing the horizon within a few miles of our start. The day's events were like the day before as we drove down the road, except the smell of the salve was gone from my body. The pain in my back was worse, as I thought about how this would be the last day on this convoy. I must have twisted my back last night, I kept thinking to myself. I couldn't remember clearly the events of the night before. I did log the events in my notes to write my letters with, but my mind was working on other things than the notes by now. The inventory paper work came to my attention, so I checked it. The unusual event of the day was when one of the other trucks got a flat tire around noon. We stopped for lunch at that time for repairs. The c-rations tasted pretty good this time I thought as I watched the men change the tire. The men seemed to be in a rush when changing the tire as they wanted to get back on the road. This confused me, because up to this point the men were slow to do anything. I placed one of my hands on the rifle in a defensive motion. I had my driver help me tighten the ace bandage that held the board to my back as we stood there. I realized a few minutes later the reason for the rush at lunch. After the convoy started down the road not a hundred yards we turned a sharp corner. There as we turned the corner the other sixteen trucks parked on the side of the road were waiting for us.

The convoy of twenty-one trucks was back together again for the final few miles of the trip. The convoy went on for about three hours, when my driver pointed to the base ahead. The truck that I was in now led the convoy, stopping at the main gate to complete our mission. I got out of the truck at the main gate and reported to the Sergeant of the Guard. I at that time had the Sergeant sign a receipt for the paper work before I would give it to him. I then was taken by jeep to a helicopter pad and flown back to the Royal Thai Air Force Base in Ubonn.

The helicopter landed on the flight line right near the MABS unit. I walked to my shop and reported back to the base operation by phone. The next week or so I did nothing except lay around my hooch and write letters. I wrote notes in my facts book, of all the things that I wanted to remember from the notes I wrote while in the truck. I couldn't remember what a lot of the notes meant by this time. I would make the notes at the time the event happen because later on these notes would cause me to recall the event I hoped. The only fact I could remember at this time was the girls placing the board on my back. My mind would flash to different events stored in my mind unexpectedly at times as thing happen. I could not remember anything until a word or situation happening around me triggered my hidden thoughts. The relief I got from the board made an impression on me that seem to stick in my thoughts. I would put the board under my ace bandage for my trip to the chow tent. Maybe that is why the memory stayed with me. The pain in my back was constant but the muscle spasms lessened as time went on.

Chapter Fifteen No Intimidation

Sitting around the hooch because of my back pain was causing me to ask serious questions about life and the reason for it. I would ask questions to myself. My mind was growing after the set back of the car accident in New Hampshire. I was developing thoughts and asking questions, as a child might do as he grows into an adult. I would think of stories of life back in the world that I heard other men talk about. Could life really be better than life that existed around me? Was what I did on the convoy my job, or should I have died instead? I am a Marine nothing can defeat me. Ignore the pain and get up and do your job. These thoughts kept echoing in my head. I took a walk to the MABS shop as a way to pass the time and get out of my hooch.

Once at the shop, I learned just how short handed the unit was in manpower at this time. The crew on the runway consisted of three men with no NCO to lead them. The Master Sergeant, when he saw me walking, ordered that I supervise the runway crew for the landing of a squad of F-4's due in from a mission. On the runway a few minutes later I introduced myself to the crew. I found that I already knew two of the men from around the shop. I had not worked with them before but I knew they had worked a few busy nights. They had experience with their jobs. The third crewmember was a private strait from school, and I had no idea what to expect from him. The hours continued to pass as we waited for the inbound aircraft. The "newbe" was placed on the far gear away from the tower phone. Practice was what this newbe needed before the hooks started so we kept going over dry runs.

The tower phone rang alerting the crew the real event was due to start soon. A squad of eleven birds was due in thirty minutes. The description of the planes on approach was that all were low on fuel. Two of the planes also had hung ordnance that is bombs that did not drop when the pilot released them. The crew placed the boots under the deck pennant at this time as the start of preparation for a hook. All engines were started and warmed up in the normal procedure for the hooks. The last thing to do was send the point man out to his position. This is the man that signals the pilot after the hook is complete. I suggested the Lance Corporal take the night wands with him, as he would be the point man. It was still daylight, but this mission could take hours to complete. Tower was advised we were ready to receive the planes. Now we waited for the squad of F-4's to come home.

Tower phone rings to advise of the F-4's on final approach. All the men jump every time the phone rings. This time was no different. I advised the men of the status of the birds on approach. One F-4 has its left landing gear up, one has its right landing gear up, two of the planes have hung ordinance and all are low on fuel. The tower would set the order of the planes to land by the fuel supply of each. The gear and the men were ready for the operation to begin.

I advised the tower that I needed to know in advance when the planes with the missing landing gear were to land. Tower agreed to my request as they advised me of the first plane on final approach. The first plane landed and cleared the runway with no problems. The tower phone rang to advise that the second plane on approach had its right landing gear up. This plane when it hooked would close the runway until it was cleared away. The tower wanted to crash this plane into the barriers at the end of the runway. This plane could remain at the end of the runway until the operation ended. This way the runway would not have to close. I advised the tower we could catch the plane and clear the runway at the same time, just to bring the F-4 in. Tower put the injured F-4 on final approach as we prepared the gear.

The absorber has different brake setting for each type of plane that hooks. The F-4 is heavy so the setting is high on the brake adjustment to give more resistance. I released the F-4 setting on the right absorber and reset it at A-4 for less braking. My hopes were that this would brake enough to stop the plane but not rip the gear out of the ground. I thought if one absorber broke faster than the other that would hold the wing in the air long enough for the plane to stop. The plane would be pulled to one side, I hoped in the grassy area off the runway. The thought was a good one except my mind did not under stand the repercussions if I was wrong.

The plane came in and hooked the deck pennant after the wheels were on the runway surface. The normal way is to hook the cable as the wheels hit the runway surface, but that slams the plane on to its landing gear hard. This landing with the right landing gear up was perfect for these conditions. The plane came to a stop before the wing touched the ground about fifteen feet clear of the runway on the grass. The next four landings were picture perfect landings. One plane after another hooked and cleared the runway. The seventh was the one with the left landing gear up.

I again changed the settings on the absorber. This time I changed the setting on the opposite absorber as the one for the last F-4 with its right landing gear up. This plane came in for a smooth landing stopping off the opposite side of the runway on the grass. We had four planes left to land. The next plane to land would be with hung ordinance making it dangerous. These hooks can be simple landings if the ordinance doesn't come loose from the wing of the plane. The problem is some times the ordinance falls off when the plane hooks from the jarring effect of the quick stop. The point man has seconds to jump out of the way of this bouncing bomb. The ordinance is a large chunk of explosive metal traveling at three to five hundred knots. This makes it difficult to avoid.

The F-4 was on final approach for landing. Everyone on the crew was ready as the planes hook snagged the deck pennant. The point man started running out on to the runway to signal the pilot with directions. The wands or flashing lights were on to signal the pilot to release his brakes. I noticed an object skidding down the runway about the same time as the point man was running out. The point man went down to a still position lying on the deck. It appeared that the ordinance went clear over the point man and off the side of the runway. The retrieve engine operator was quickly out of his pit and starting to run and assist the point man. I stopped him before he could get too far down the runway. "No," I said, "do your job!" Then I called tower and waved off the remaining three planes.

I worked my way out to point position on the runway in a full run. The pain in my back was there but I was adjusting my mind to accept it. The point man was breathing but lying dazed in a pool of blood. I leaned down to roll him off the runway as quickly as I could. My body collapsed to my knees with pain. I used my hands, arms and body to roll this object off the edge of the runway. I stood up half way and signaled the engine operator to clear with tower to land the remaining planes.

An F-4 was on final approach as I gave the clear signal to the tower phone operator. The plane appeared that it was close enough to the gear that it would have to be waved off one more time. This plane I learned later had planed to crash into the barriers at the end of the runway. Our clearing at the last second must have changed the pilot's mind. The plane dropped the hook just in time to catch the deck pennant, which surprised us all. The remaining planes must be really low on fuel for tower to be bringing them in without our signal clearing the gear. That is how I justified the non-communication on the tower's part in my head, as we were about to finish up the last of the landings.

I had taken up a position about fifteen to twenty feet on the runway. I never moved from that spot after moving the injured point man off the runway. The normal way is a plane hooks and the point man runs to this assumed spot signaling the pilot on his way onto the runway. I could hardly move because of the pain in my back so I decided to just stand out on the runway and do the job from that spot. I thought that if I died the pain would be gone, so why worry about a plane hitting me? Each time a plane landed and hooked, I could signal the pilot and the plane could pick up its hook without my moving. The pennant cleared the hook on the first landing, as I signaled the engine operators to retrieve the cable.

The next plane landed and hooked the gear within a second of the boots being placed under the deck pennant. This particular plane must have passed within inches of the boot chaser head as I watched from my position. The F-4 hooked and came to a stop about fifty feet from my position. I did all the signals as required to free the plane from the deck pennant and still never moved from my position. The plane was cleared by my signal and started off the runway to the taxiway. I was signaling the engine operators to retrieve the deck pennant when I noticed the last F-4 in the squad was on final approach. The tower phone was too far away for me to reach it and the engine operators were busy. The cable was being pulled tight as the hook on the next plane hit the runway within six inches of the deck pennant. The hook bounced over the deck pennant because the boots were not under it to lift the cable up. I quickly signaled the pilot by flashing the wands (from the ground into the sky) to go back up into the air. The F-4 pilot picked the nose of his plane high in the air and hit the plane's afterburners. The F-4 looked like a rocket taking off from a launch pad at NASA. The thrust of an F-4's exploding within fifty feet of my position ripped my sound suppressors off my head. I flew as the force of the after burners hit me about two hundred feet down the runway. I landed in a deep puddle of water on the edge of the flight line. I scrambled to my feet. I was too far down the runway for a point man to do his job but I could still signal the pilot and hope he saw the wands. I made it to the edge of the runway and started slowly walking back toward the gear. I watched the F-4 on final approach as I painfully struggled to walk back down the edge of the runway. The pilot hooked but I was still too far out of position to do my job. The plane stopped and I saw it roll back as the hook went up, clearing the gear. The engine operators must have retrieved the gear for a short distance as if I had signaled them. The plane must have raised the hook as a normal response to a hook landing. I signaled the pilot from far down the runway to exit the runway. He taxied away so he was cleared from the gear and headed to the hangers. I do not believe my signals had any effect on the performance of my men or the pilot on that landing, but out of habit I still did them.

The engine operators retrieved the gear. They then shut everything down and cleared tower to be on a standby status. The runway was closed anyway so that the F-4s that had gone off the runway could be removed. I made it back to the injured point man who was still off the side of the runway as fast as I could. I got there just after my crew had arrived in the area. The two-crew men were mad that I left the point man without help while we did our jobs. In a dazed voice the point man muttered, "What happened?" After a short time the dazed man explained how the ordinance went over his head scaring the daylight out of him. The last thing he remembered was ducking so quickly he hit his head on the deck. All the blood came from a small abrasion on the side of his head about the size of a dime. The runway was down so the four of us helped each other back to the shop.

That crew shift ended as we reached the shop, so we were finished work for a time. It was 0730 hours after I walked out to the shop. I was sore, tired and in a lot of pain at this point. I remember taking a long time walking back to my hooch. I walked past the shower and decided that the time wasted walking to my hooch and back would be crazy. I took all my clothes off and stacked them on a rock. I found the remains of a bar of soap stuck behind the showerhead pipe and retrieved it. I washed my body several times, not because of the dirt but because the water felt good as it bounced off my body. I then picked up my clothes and walked back to the hooch nude and wet. I woke up twenty-four hours later not knowing where I was or what was going on. I laid on my cot until I could put my thoughts together. I then realized I was a Marine stationed in Thailand.

I felt a lot better even though the pain in my back was still there. I headed to the shop to see if I had the day off or was assigned duty. I opened the door to go in the shop and the Master Sergeant was right in my face. "Destroying two F-4s, boy you're in deep trouble," he said to me. The CO came into the room and said, "Leaving an injured man on the side of the runway without help, Sergeant," as he joined the conversation. The two openly discussed how I would get so much time in the brig people would forget who I was. I looked at the two men straight in the eyes. The intimidation I might have felt before was gone. The feeling, emotions, intimidation, no longer existed in me. I in a command voice stated "These are my men, my gear, my situation. I had to make decisions. I did the job the best way I saw fit. The F-4s hooked and stopped. The point man was down. Marines die. I do not stop my mission because I lost one man, Sir." The conversation was interrupted. Two Marine pilots were standing behind me. The shop Commandeering Officer called the room to attention.

The pilots must have heard the conversation as they approached the shop. They placed us at ease and then one of the pilots told how the unit had done an impossible job, catching the eleven planes without loosing one pilot. He complemented the Captain and the Master Sergeant for training such an efficient crew. The two pilots both told how they would like to thank the crew personally, but they didn't have time for that. The pilots left the area as quickly as they entered. I was dismissed back to my hooch until I received orders.

The Master Sergeant from the shop appeared at my door about an hour later. He knocked once then walked into my hooch and sat in the chair. I was lying on the cot as the Master Sergeant started telling me a story. The Marine Corps is made up of some pretty brave men, the Master Sergeant said. Some Marines don't live up to there potential. Others exceed it. You do dumb things but the way you stood and defended your actions, you are a Marine in my book. Then in the same tone of voice he told me a plane leaves at 1600 hours and be on it. The Master Sergeant was half way out the door when he turned and said, "Don't worry about the Commanding officer, the pressure gets to him." The plane left with me on it for Clark Air Force Base that very day.

Chapter sixteen: Staff Sergeant

I landed in Iwakuni, Japan that day only a few hours after leaving Clark Air Force Base in the Philippines. I had a feeling that I had been on this base before but was not sure. My mind was a blank, as far as recognizing any of the buildings or other features that identified the base. People sometimes told me I said or did something that I did not recall. Maybe this was one of those "de'ja vo" times. I would assume these individuals were telling me the truth and brush it off unless it affected my life. If it involved money or work, I would assess the situation and take the action I thought best. I often had these feelings that I had been a place before. I never really knew one way or the other. I rationalized that it looked similar to some other place I had been, and write it off. I just accepted the fact I did not remember things the way other people did. I was always bumping into people who knew me quite well, but I could not recall ever meeting them. To avoid explaining why I did not remember, I learned to pretend with general responses. I accepted the fact that some things I remembered as if they were printed in my mind. Some things I didn't remember at all. Other parts of my lost memory I recalled by hearing certain words or phrase that could bring a fact out of my memory. Each situation was different. A lost memory was something I didn't know was lost, so I did not miss not remembering.

So as far as I was concerned this was a new assignment, on a new base. I caught the flight line passenger bus to the base administration office for the check in process to begin. I asked the bus driver for some information on the name of the admission clerk. This would make check in easier on this base if I knew who to go to. The check in process at this base turned out to be simple for the rank of a sergeant. We just signed a few forms and got told to which unit we are assigned. In a matter of minutes it was back to the flight line for me on the base bus. My assignment was the MABS unit located out on the flight line where I had just come from.

Most of the men in the unit were "newbe;" even the Commanding officer had rotated in the past six months. Therefore I did not know anyone in the unit that I recognized as I was introduced. A Staff Sergeant seemed to know me but never actually said anything to me to confirm or not confirm the feeling. He had recently been promoted from sergeant to Staff Sergeant, but I did not remember the base, never mind him, so that fact did not help. I moved on to the next task at hand.

The unit assigned me to runway duty with a nine-man crew. Rules and discipline in this unit were well defined. Crews mustered each morning at 0600 hours on the days of their shift. At that time the crew would use "5.0" the runway truck for a chow run, then back to the shop. The crew was a team, which meant all or nobody went to chow. There was no splitting the crew. After chow, the crew was transported to the runway shack no later than 0730 hours. All runway gear was checked first thing in the morning. The engines started, and tested, pressures and equipment performance standards logged in a book. The men were required to have all PM (primary maintenance) done by the 1200 hours chow run. The runway truck would arrive with bag lunches at precisely that time. If the maintenance was not done the chow hour was shortened. The crew at 1300 hours did practice drills, running to the gear, and set ups to receive a hook. After all drills were completed to required performance levels the runway gear would be put back to ready status. Physical fitness training would begin at 1400 hours and continue for two hours at a set level of performance. The unit Commanding officer would inspect the runway shack at 1630 hours each day, which gave the crew from 1600 to 1630 to make the shack spotless. Dinner would arrive at 1730 hours each evening by way of the runway truck (5.0) delivery. A crewmember was assigned to return the "5.0" driver back to the shop and return to the shack with the truck. After chow the crew was allowed free time to do as they wished while on emergency ready status. The majority of the men wrote letters while watching television. The shack was well furnished with couches and a nice color television for the crew's relaxation. This was the furniture that less than one year earlier I had removed from the senior NCO's television room. I had no memory or even being on this base before. I was impressed with the excellent condition of the furniture, but did not remember my part in obtaining it. The remaining crew if not writing would read books or sleep whatever they wished. It was the individual's choice. The crew would remain on ready status at the shack until the runway shut down for the night. After the runway shut down the crew would go back to the sleep quarters at the unit shop on stand by status until morning muster.

There was a clearly defined structure to the policy in this unit. I was impressed with the Marine Corps structure and performance of this unit. I introduced myself as Sergeant Macdonald to my crew as I told them what to expect. Telling the men I was their crew leader and that they had jobs to do was a fact the men knew but it needed to be said by me. It sounded like I was giving a generic government speech to the men when I next stated these jobs were to be done and done right the first time. This was clearly instilled in the crew. I was their leader. In the introduction, I informed the men that I take crap from no one. I am their Sergeant and I expect them to follow procedure. I told them if they have a problem they come to me with it. If I can help with the problem I will or I will see the chain of command is followed until their problem is solved. I told the men I would learn the unit protocol over the next few weeks. If they toy with me in the beginning, look out after I learn. I told the men at the end of the introduction to go do their jobs. Dismissed. In some way I had changed. My attitude or maybe my direction had achieved it's own personality. I no longer accepted myself as good enough for anyone back in the world to associate with. I stopped writing letters to everyone. I no longer read my mail. Each letter I placed in my footlocker unopened. For some reason I became depressed and unable to communicate with non-military personnel. I was a Marine Sergeant with a job to do.

I had a good crew as my new assignment started. Over the next few weeks I got to know each one of the men individually. I did not become their friend, but I became someone they could talk to about anything. I personally had never been married. Heck, I never planned to get married. I didn't even know if I had ever had a relationship with a girl, or if anything happened if I had had a relationship. One of the hardest discussions I would have with any crewmember was when one of the men got a dear john letter. I was someone who had no memory. Yet I was giving advice on subjects I knew nothing about.

I was at this point having trouble hearing people's voices when they talked. I could hear some words clearly as the person spoke. I first noticed this hearing problem in my final days in Thailand. If the person changed the tone in their voice, the words would become distorted or silent to me. I learned to compensate by asking, How do you feel? What do you think? What would you do? Those kinds of questions to the men in place of talking with them. The men always left the conversation feeling better, but I never told them what to do. My crew in a way was good for me also because it got me to thinking about women and relationships.

My crew shift on one particular day had ended. I took a walk to the PX, which is a store on base. I saw this little, skinny guy with short black hair struggling to get a box in a car. The box looked heavy, so I started to help him with a friendly hand. I reached over the open passenger's side door and grabbed the edge of the box. The man and I slid the box easily into the car. Thinking the box was heavy was the reason that I got involved. I started to apologize because I may have insulted this Japanese man by my actions. The box may have looked heavy but it was not. I looked down into the prettiest face that was looking back at me. I finished saying, "I sorry," and added the introductory line, "I am Sergeant Macdonald". This girl looked familiar to me. I just knew I had met her someplace before. She told me her name was Kimko, but she was late for work at the base bookstore and had to leave.

Kimko was on my mind all that night. I knew her. Or was my mind taking a thought of someone I met earlier in my life that looks like her, and making me believe it was Kimko? The next day it was off to the bookstore for me. I had to check this dream girl out once again. I did not like to read books. I had trouble remembering what a paragraph said when I was finished reading it. Reading books trying to retain the information from one paragraph to the next made me forget more job and life related things. On my correspondence courses I would highlight important facts. I just looked up the answers whenever I took a test. The courses were helping me because unexpectedly facts would pop into my thoughts when I needed to solve a related problem while doing a job. The bookstore was only the size of a large closet. This closet was filled with books completely from the floor to the ceiling. Kimko was the only person in the bookstore as I walked through the door. She recognized my face from the day before. This helped break the ice of the introduction. Our conversation filled a half-hour visit, which started a bond developing between us. A customer interrupted the interaction at that point. I talked Kimko into having lunch with me that day before I left the store. I told her I knew a cook at the mess hall that I would bring lunch for the both of us. She answered by telling me she would think of me until lunch.

I made a couple ham and cheese subs at the mess hall before meeting Kimko out side the book store. Some chips, milk, cups of pudding and the subs filled a backpack in my hand. I left the mess hall and walked the hundred yards up the street to meet Kimko as she came out of the bookstore. We didn't go far from the store just to a picnic table across the street that was vacant. Kimko was so easy to talk with which made me relax and enjoy her beauty. I felt more than ever we had been friends for years. The time for lunch passed by too quickly, as a desire to be with this girl filled my every wish. We had to say good bye, but Kimko added, "You very friendly person," as she crossed the road back to the bookstore. I knew that seeing her again was a must, but my shift at work started the next day. The food and Kimko's company put a warm friendly feeling in my body.

My work shifts were mapped out as what would be done all day long. The time allowed to vary from the list meant less time to perform the required tasks. Practice drills were a lesson that was required each day to prepare the men for all situations. The real plane catching the gear was a better experience for the lesson at least in my mind. I tried for two real hooks a day to give the men a real feel for the action. I worked with my men every day that our shift was on duty. I would do the work with the men doing the actual jobs. We worked together on every event as a team. I could show the men what I expected. My working with the men allowed me the hands on demonstration versus trying to recall from my memory. While we were working the men would express their ideas back. We would discuss the better solution, outcomes of the different ideas. I didn't always accept their idea, but I made a point to listen and discuss their thoughts with them. I used listening as a tool to deflect my lack of memory from the men. The hands on method allowed my recall system to draw information from that trapped reservoir of information in my head. The only way to extract it was by some key word or event opening that page up for my mind to read. Kimko's page was open on my mind and I thought about her my entire shift.

My next day off I went to the bookstore around lunchtime and surprised Kimko. I advised her that I had packed a lunch and would appreciate it if she would share it with me. She had a shy reaction. She looked at the deck and softly said, "I was hoping you come back". I felt good talking with her about any subject. After that day on my off time from work we would get together for walks. Natural feelings of joy for both of us to just walk and talk made our days together fun. Our hands or bodies would brush each other once in a while by accident. We became good friends to each other. On one of our walks, we met Kimko's friend who was driving a motor cycle that was for sale. In the conversation that soon started I learned this friend was selling her bike for nine thousand yen (twenty-five dollars). I still had the money I saved from when I chased the prisoner. I thought to myself about that money and maybe using some of it. So after talking to Kimko about if she liked bikes, I brought the bike while at the bookstore that day.

I worked the next day with only part of my crew on the runway. The shift was pretty much normal for runway traffic until the fifteen hundred hour. We had an A-6e coming in on an emergency of possible stuck throttle and maybe hung ordinance. The ETA was sixty minutes. My men all knew which position to take because I assigned them at morning muster. Each day the men would get a different position for learning purposes. I logged every man and his position in the runway logbook so there would be a record of who did what. This log also helped me in that I needed a tool for remembering who was where. This workday we were short handed. This would mean the men left on the runway crew would have to work faster to get all the work done on time.

The crew at this time was a four-man crew plus myself. A memo asking for temporary help at the base supply got some of the men TAD for the day.

I saw no need to inform the unit shop of the emergency approach. I had worked many hours in the past with fewer men on my crew during worst crisis. I approached this as a routine emergency with more or less the required manpower. I had two engine operators, a boot runner, a point man and myself on tower phone. I gave the green light to the tower. I had the images of being on the runway in Thailand flashing in my head.

The A-6e was ten minutes out. My men were in position waiting for the plane to go on final approach. I had two Lance Corporals running the retrieve engines. A PFC was running boots and the "newbe" private was out at the point. Across the taxiway I could see the "5.0" truck headed toward the gear. As the truck got closer I could see the shop Staff Sergeant was the only person in the truck. I heard on the tower phone that "5.0" was clearing through the tower to cross at midpoint on the runway. After crossing the runway "5.0" stopped beside me near the tower phone for a minute. The Staff Sergeant started to ask "if I needed" but stopped in mid sentence. The truck took off toward the point position down the side of the runway. I could hear the Staff Sergeant yell, "how can you have a private on point?" I ordered the engine operator to take the tower phone and listen for the A-6e approach.

The truck stopped about fifty feet off the runway at a position even with the point man. I reached the point position just as the Staff Sergeant was relieving the private from his assigned job. I stopped the private and ordered him back in position for the plane on approach. I then told the Staff Sergeant, "This is my crew, my runway and you are to get the hell off it." The Staff Sergeant pointed to the stripes on his shirt and started to pull rank. I planted a punch right on the end of the Staff Sergeant's nose in what one might call a flash reaction. The Staff Sergeant went out like a light as he collapsed to the ground. The pain in my back brought my body to snap up straight. I felt as if a knife was being twisted into my body real slow. I had just thrown my back into muscle spasms at the most inopportune time. The private helped me put the Staff Sergeant into the benjo ditch (a Japanese drainage ditch). I then took the tower phone operation over from the radio on "5.0". I cleared the A-6e for a hook, as it was still one minute away. The plane hooked with no problem and the gear was readied for stand by status.

The Staff Sergeant was lying in the ditch holding his nose. The private and I walked back to the runway shack to prepare for the 1630-hour inspection. When the inspection was being done, the Commanding Officer informed me that disciplinary action was being filed against me. The remainder of the shift for the next twenty-four hours was uneventful. During the free time that evening the men were inquisitive about how bad the situation was for me, but I had no answer. At the morning muster there was an order for me to report to the unit Commanding Officer's office after my crew was dismissed.

When the morning muster was completed, I reported to the unit Commanding Officer's office as ordered. I sat across the room in the administration office from the Staff Sergeant. His nose was red. I stared at him with unforgiving eyes just to irritate him. I could tell it was getting to him because he was taking short peeks to see I was still looking in his direction. At least an hour passed, and my mind pretty much forgot the reason I was sitting there. The Commanding Officer finally walked into the building and ordered the Staff Sergeant and I into his office. We stood front and center at attention at the Commanding Officer's desk. The Commanding Officer began speaking about the stack of charges here on these pages, as he placed several papers on his desk. The Staff Sergeant or myself gave no response because we were still at attention. The Commanding Officer ordered the Staff Sergeant to lay out the bases for such charges.

The Staff Sergeant started out that he was at an E-6 pay grade. He went on to explain in the uniform code of military justice that senior grade tell junior grade what to do. The junior grade obeys orders with out question. I purposely disobeyed his orders superceding what he ordered a private to do. I then struck a senior NCO with my fist. The charges and explanation continued one after another until finally the Commanding Officer sat back in his chair. A minute or two later the Commanding Officer's mouth opened but his lips never moved as he asked for my answer to the charges. I responded "Sir, everything the Staff Sergeant says is true." The Commanding Officer told us to think about the consequences of the charges. He then informed us the hearing would be in one week. Dismissed.

I had the day off to spend with Kimko. My bike was now registered and I had my international motorcycle license issued to me by this time. I could now drive on and off any base that I wished. Kimko and I had decided to spend the day in a village named Onta. It was located about fifty kilometers north east of the base. The day was sunny and warm as Kimko sat behind me on the bike. Her arms being wrapped around my waist made me feel good about life. She would rest her chin on my shoulder and sing Japanese songs in my ear as we traveled on the bike. Every time I hit a bump our helmets would clang like a drum beating off tune. The day was perfect as we enjoyed each stop on the route we took.

The traffic right from the main gate of the base to the first city was stop and go. There seemed to be more people and vehicles than space to move in. On a few occasions I was able to move past cars that had stopped to let people cross in front of them. The distance we traveled in one hour was less than five kilometers. The time didn't matter to me though, because I felt happy and warm with Kimko's arms wrapped around me. The desire to complete the mission of reaching our destination made my body want to move but traffic dictated how fast we could travel. My mind worked on single thoughts. The goal of the day was to get to a certain point on the map. This thought of completing a mission made my body impulsive, but the traffic did not corporate.

Kimko wanted to stop for awhile and walk around as traffic was at a standstill. I could now see the people up close and listen to them talk as we walked. The language being spoken was strange sounding to me. I had heard Japanese spoken before many times in Japan and Okinawa. The difference was the number of people speaking at once. I did not hear one American voice in the air, and I felt isolated. The feeling of seeing and hearing everything going on around me made me think I was the only American left. This was strange for me. I talked to Kimko about my feelings on what was happening. She seemed to understand about what I meant in my talk with her. I on the other hand wasn't sure that I understood. Kimko explained how when she was little, she would go to work with her father at the base mess hall. She would sit for hours reading books while her father cleaned the dishes. The room would be filled with Americans speaking in a language she did not understand. She decided to learn English as a way to understand what was happening around her. Kimko suggested she teach me Japanese for the same reason. I told her that would be nice. The first words Kimko taught me in Japanese were "wait a minute." I had learned these words while in Okinawa but didn't tell Kimko. So as not to discourage her.

We stopped at a few stores as we walked around the city on our adventure. Kimko would thumb through the racks of records, clothes or whatever looking interested in what was there. The clerk would come up to her and something would click between the two to them. The body language between Kimko and the clerk would start to get obvious. The talk as the hands and arms would move making the discussion look like acting. It would appear the two would get into a heated argument as they negotiated. Kimko would throw her hands up in the air and walk away in disgust. This would indicate she had finished the bargaining process. Finally after three stores I asked her if she knows all these people that she bargain with. This caused her to look at me with a smile on her face. She told me she likes to play a game while shopping. Kimko went on to explain how you ask, what is the price of an item. Then you belittle what ever it is that you are pretending to buy. The clerk will defend the item that was on sale and insist on the asking price. At that point you offer a small part of the price for the item. The clerk can accept the price in which case you walk away. The clerk gets mad and yells at you but no matter what the clerk says to you: you throw your hands up in the air and walk away. She told me how she learned this as a child in school, with her friends for fun. The shopping went on for a couple of hours before we moved on with our trip. The city took a while longer to negotiate through on the bike. We eventually got on to the open roads into the country.

I could not believe the countryside of Japan. There were colorful hills with plowed fields and trees all around. The sky was clear so we could see miles over the hillsides, enjoying their beauty. This must have been farm country because there were large open areas for planted crops. Japanese style structures dotted the countryside around the fields. My mind dreamed this scene was a beautiful picture framed on a wall. The cliffs of the steep mountains filled the background of my picture with a brown gray color. I stopped the bike to enjoy the scene with Kimko by my side.

Kimko started explaining what we were looking at on the mountainside. We sat side by side on the seat of the bike with our bodies resting against each other. Kimko would point to an area and tell me "that is a temple where these people have prayer. That over there is a rich person's house that owns a factory in the city." Night darkness was now coming into the talk between us. Kimko began telling how night is almost here and we should go. We talked about how we still had to negotiate our way back through the city to the base in order complete the day. The distance we had traveled out of the only city we had passed through on that day was not that far. The traffic would bog us down quickly as we enter the city, but it did not matter.

The ride was pleasant with the cool night air blowing in our faces. Dark of night created shadows from the glare of the lights that masked the poor standards of the populations living condition. The crowds of people and traffic still filled every inch of space, but we continued to move forward toward the base. Kimko's soft voice singing Japanese songs in my ear and her arms wrapped tight around my waist relaxed me. I was beginning to feel at peace about myself. I felt like someone needed me as a part of them. I belonged where I was. I looked up and realized that very moment we just entered the street to the main gate of the base. I had no memory of the trip up to that point. I stopped the bike at a store just out side the base's main gate.

The hour was past 2300 hours. I thought it was too late for Kimko to walk home alone and be safe. I asked if I could drive her home, so I would feel sure she would get safely there. Her words were strong, that driving her home would not be right. I knew Kimko loved to eat ice cream sandwiches. I asked her to compromise with me on the subject. I would buy each of us an ice cream sandwich in return she would let me walk her home. The tired twinkle in her eyes assured me I had won the discussion. We slowly walked toward her house talking and laughing with each other. Her house was closer than I had realized. She lived just one street away from the main gate.

Kimko turned toward me to say good night. She placed her arms around my neck to give me a hug. I looked into her eyes and I felt this tingling need in my body. She must have felt the same feelings at that time as I did. Her head tilted up wards in a way that asked me to kiss her. I could see her lips become moist as the street light glistened of pink color with a shine that acted as an invitation. I then heard a voice speaking Japanese close behind me. Kimko jumped one step back in disbelief. I turned to look at who was speaking. Kimko reaction made me some how know the words that came were from her father. A noise came out of my mouth as I stood in shock, "Hoo?" I saw Kimko's father within an arm's length of where we were standing as I turned to look back.

Kimko's father looked just as shocked as I did. He stood next to Kimko holding her hand. "Corporal?" The father asked in an open statement to whoever wanted to answer. I assumed Kimko talked about me and that was how he knew who I was. I soon learned that was not the case. Kimko blurted out in English, "You know?" Kimko's father shook my hand as if we were old friends. I had no idea what was going on, but I played along and asked the question, "How have you been?" The man started to talk when Kimko asked again, "you know?" Kimko's father told a story about how a Marine truck driver left a truckload of goods at the mess hall to be unloaded. He was getting off work but could not leave until the truck was empty. The boxes were heavy and he had trouble moving them. He told Kimko I was walking by and stopped to help him. As he told the story I could remember something about a truck and helping but not when or where. It was like dreams appearing in my mind as I listened to Kimko's father tell the story. I didn't know if I remembered it because it happened or because I related it to something else. Could Kimko's father just be associating the event with me and it was another Marine that did the work? Maybe I looked like someone that Kimko's father thinks helped him. The hour was late. After a few more minutes we said good night.

I had the runway shift that morning and I had to be at muster on time. The time was after 0200 hours when I arrived at the barracks after leaving Kimko and her father. 0730 muster was normal for me that morning as everything seemed typical. I had no memory of the problems that I got into on my shift before this shift. The talk and words of the men on how this skinny little Sergeant knocked the Staff Sergeant out cold made the event come back to me. I wrote everything that flashed in my mind down in notes on a pad. The shop was tense every time that I walked through it. I couldn't picture what the discussions were between the men as relating to me. I knew what the men were saying did relate to me but was it real. The crew and I started out to the runway on our normal routine. I forgot all about the problems by the time we got to the shack and the day was like any other day to me. I would think of the situation when some one asked me if I was worried about the disciplinary hearing. Most of the time I didn't know about the problem because it wasn't on my mind. I would forget it moments after someone talked about it. The way my appearance did not let my problem interfere or even show amazed the men. I was beginning to understand the fact that I didn't retain thoughts like other men did.

My workdays and time off came and went with no out of the ordinary excitement. I saw Kimko at the bookstore several times but I was too busy with laundry and other things to go on any trips with her. Kimko was busy also but she did tell me one day at the bookstore that her father wanted me to come for a dinner at her house. The shift before my disciplinary hearing was just about over. I held off answering Kimko about dinner. I had not even thought about what the results of this hearing might do to me. After morning muster, the Gunny advised me that the hearing was at 0900. "Do not be late" were the

Gunny's last words to me. I went back to the barracks to take a shower and put on a fresh work uniform. I took the papers with my notes on it and started reading them in the hopes of remembering the situation. The more times I read the notes, the stronger my belief grew about what had happened. I convinced myself from the notes that what the Sergeant in the story did was right. I was like a third person looking in on someone else's problem.

The Staff Sergeant was in the chair by the Commanding Officer's office door waiting for the 0900 hour to come. I entered the room. I walked up to the table, filled a cup half full of coffee, and started talking to the Staff Sergeant in a friendly manner. I felt no emotion about what was going on because on my part there was nothing personal. I read the facts on a piece of paper. The whole situation was like a story in a book. You like or dislike the story and you can defend the book or not. To take offence and show emotion about a story would interfere with your job. The Staff Sergeant took offence at the fact I could be so casual about what was going on. I had no understanding of why he felt that way but I could accept he must have had a bad night. I just did and acted like what was normal for me until the door opened at 0900 hours. The Staff Sergeant snapped up to attention at that very moment. I smiled at the same time as I set my cup down on the Staff Sergeant's desk and walked into the Commanding Officer's office.

The two Marines stood rigidly at attention in front of the Commanding Officer's desk and reported in. The Staff Sergeant went first and explained how that when I was stationed in this unit before I was a troublemaker. He justified his keeping a close watch on my performance because of his duty to the unit and the Corps. The Staff Sergeant then went on to explain he heard the emergency call on the tower radio. He knew most of my men were TAD for the day from my crew. He headed out to the runway to see if my crew needed help. The first thing he noticed was that the "newbe" private was running the point position. He said that he drove to where I was standing to advise me to replace the private. The tower signaled over the radio that the emergency A-6e was on final. He looked down the runway to notice the private was out of position by at least one hundred feet. He went on to say as a senior NCO on site he assessed the situation and took action. He drove the truck to the point position and was about to order the private off the runway. The Sergeant (myself) appeared at the same time that he was about to give the private the orders. The Staff Sergeant went on to say that he ordered the Sergeant back to the gear at that moment. He said before another word was spoke the Sergeant struck him in the face

The Commanding Officer looked at me and said, "Sergeant, is that the way it happened?" I was still at attention. In a clear voice I stated, "Yes sir." The Commanding Officer looked at the Gunny sitting in a chair beside where I was standing. I heard the Gunny speaking but because I was still at attention I could not turn to see him. After he finished asking if I could justify my actions, I heard in my head the familiar saying, "Marines do their job and die." The Gunny asked again "Why did you that)? I clearly spoke with only my lips moving, "These are my men, my planes, no one interferes with them. They speak to me first. The Staff Sergeant was an object in my way. I eliminated it to perform my job Sir." The Commanding Officer stood up leaned over his desk and put his face right in front of mine.

The Commanding Officer started yelling at me from his first word, "Sergeant these are my men, my runway, and my planes. You are mine. No one disrupts the flow of my unit. You are relieved of duty on the runway. Your new job is Supply Sergeant." He then looked at the Staff Sergeant and said. "You're to take over the runway crew. Dismissed!"

Chapter Seventeen: Cherry Blossoms

My new job was to start the same day that I was taken off of runway duty. I had never worked in supply before that I remembered, so it was something new. The Gunny not five minutes after I reached my new desk came up stairs to the supply room. "Sergeant," he said, "The Commanding Officer can't say this but I can. What you did was wrong but justified. The Commanding Officer had to do something to save face for the Staff Sergeant. That is why you are in supply. Your being here is not a punishment, but an action to show the troops what you did was wrong. The paperwork will never get in your record." He stood up as if to walk away and coldly looked down at me saying, "The Staff Sergeant is a kiss ass, but why do you do such dumb things?" I just smiled as the Gunny walked away. This job was great for me, I thought to my self. I now worked eight hours a day, with weekends off. I could now spend weekends with Kimko.

I liked my new job from the moment it began. I started organizing the shelves as I inventoried each item. I removed every item from each shelf first. The second thing I would did was wash and polish the area before checking the code numbers off the inventory list. The process was slow because there were so many shelves and items on them. A pile of each different part was stuffed solid in every available space, I noticed. There were two thousand packages of a single kind of washer. I knew that maybe one or two of these type washers would be called for in the entire year of repairing the gear. In each step of my inventory I found waste and useless items. The government had over ordered these parts by the thousands. I continued to do my job, but kept wondering why would anyone waste so much money. The books showed an O-ring that should cost ten cents; the Marine Corps paid twenty-five dollars for it. I opened one to see what was so special about this particular O-ring. My mind recalled exactly where this particular part was called for in the assembly of an absorber. I decided it was a cheap item not worth the money they spent. As a test I pulled on the O-ring to check its strength, and it quickly broke. I put the broken O-ring in the trash and kept working.

The weekend arrived again at the end of my first week at the new job. This was a special time because I was invited to have a meal with Kimko and her family. They asked me to be at their house by mid-morning of this warm first day of spring. I was excited as I prepared for the day. I had gone to the PX and got some civilian cloths (non-military) so I would fit in with the family life. I next got on my bike and drove over to the street Kimko lived on just outside the main gate. I noticed that as I was driving down her street Kimko and her family were loading the family car.

As I stopped the bike beside him, Mr. Hoo told me this was the weekend of the Cherry Blossom festival. He said it would be a great honor if I would spend that day with the family. I was asked to get in the car by Kimko who had come out of the house a minute or so before. I opened a rear door to enter the car. Kimko told me, "In Japan, man ride in front. It is a dishonor you don't." Kimko and her mother got in the back while Mr. Hoo and I sat up front. The drive was not to long. We drove into a parking area within minutes from the time we left Kimko's house. The park was filled with a crowd of people and their supplies for a picnic. The park lawn was covered with a white blanket of cherry blossom petals.

Mr. Hoo set the blanket in a clearing between the outstretched branches of the cherry trees hanging over head. The air felt like it had been cleansed with the sweet smell of cherries. The sound of friendly chatter in a foreign language set the mood of the people who appeared to behaving a good time. I assumed each blanket was filled with family and friends. The park was filled up with in minutes of our arrival. The crowd filling the area as far as the eye could see. This instant crowed of people amazed me. The whole area was like a sea of private little islands of blankets supporting each individual family. The islands were castles of entire families to live on with the possibly to bond with each other. Kimko and her mother set the baskets and food down on the lawn. One blanket Kimko and her mother spread to create our island. The other blankets they set on the edge of our island with the food.

Kimko was dressed in a white body-tight blouse, with a light blue flared skirt, which covered the top half of her knees. The blouse and skirt were tied together with a narrow black leather belt embodied with oriental designs looping around her slim waist. Her feet were covered with little white slippers she left at the edge of the blanket before stepping onto it. The motion of her stepping on the blanket with bare feet was so graceful it was a joy to watch.

Kimko was standing about one foot from the edge of the blanket moving slowly with the music. I was about four feet away on the other side of the blanket facing her. The rays from the rising sun behind her body put an angel's glow around her. She was beautiful as she stood there. I watched as she slowly lowered herself in a winding snake like motion down to the blanket. Her skirt now covered her lower legs and feet as she reached out and fluffed some air under the skirt. The skirt settled in a circle around her as if to claim this space as hers. Kimko reached down and handed her mother a bowl of homemade cheese spread after she settled into her spot. Mother was preparing coffee and bread to serve as a snack to the men these women aimed to please.

Mother, as every one called her, had on what looked like a silk bathrobe. She was covered from head to toe with a beautiful smooth soft Japanese kimono. The Japanese print on the kimono told the story of a Samurai coming home to his loved one. These two ladies were nice to look at as they did all the work dressed like queens. I tried to help but Kimko placed her hand on top of mine while looking down at the blanket and said in a soft voice, "Please, women work." The coffee and bread were served to Mr. Hoo first then it was my turn. Kimko laid a slice of bread in both of her hands. She then extended out her arms placing her hands over my hands. She separated her hands slowly brushing the surface of my hands with the backs of hers. The bread with cheese spread on top settled into the cradle that was formed by our hands. I looked at her face, the whole time this was happening. Her eyes looked down at the blanket with her head tipped downward. The beauty of her face with the rising sun now above her head was exquisite. Her hands paused at the last moment as her moist lips formed a soft smile. I had a warm feeling in me that would last the entire day.

The day turned to evening before I was ready for this to happen. The women were cleaning up after the meal as they had done each time before.

I felt bad letting mother and Kimko do all the work. I would ask if I could help every so often. The same thing happened every time. Kimko would place her soft hands over mine and say in a soft voice, "Please, women's work". I knew she would respond in that way after the first time. This was my way of touching her in the presence of her father who was a short distance away. I think Kimko realized this because after a few times I could see that soft smile on her face appear before she touched me.

After the blanket was organized mother again reached to the corner of the blanket for a jug. Mr. Hoo had placed this gallon jug on the edge of the blanket when we arrived. The cork stuck out of the top of the jug about one inch. Mother leaned over Kimko and myself to pass the jug to Mr. Hoo. Kimko held two glasses out toward Mr. Hoo after mother returned to her spot. With a slow twist Mr. Hoo removed the cork and filled the glasses with a white wine looking juice. I drank from one glass and Mr. Hoo drank from the other. The liquid was a sharp, dry warm taste that opened your eyes wide with each sip. Mr. Hoo told me it was "Sake" Japanese wine. The two women giggled at my reaction to my first sip. They quickly looked at the blanket when Mr. Hoo's eyes caught theirs.

The hours must have passed as the jug became empty long after dark had fallen. The next thing I remember is waking up at about 0500 hours just as the sun was peeking over the horizon. I saw Mr. Hoo covered with a blanket still in the same spot as the day before. Mother lay beside him on the outside of the blanket to keep Mr. Hoo warm. I had a blanket over my body also. Close by on the outside of my blanket was Kimko. I moved my head to see where I was hoping this was not a dream. I remembered the picnic as I noticed the cherry blossom trees with a few scattered blankets of people still around in the park. Kimko must have felt me move because she quickly sat up and look around. The movement of her father at that moment made Kimko lay down on the blanket a short distance away from me. Mr. Hoo saw I was awake and said "Good morning" to me. Kimko at that moment moved in a stretching motion as if just awaking.

We laid around for another hour or so until everyone was awake. Mr. Hoo and I walked a short distance as he spoke of the traditions of his ancestors. I looked around as I listened to Mr. Hoo talk. The park was as clean as when we arrived the day before, except for the few people still sleeping. By the time Mr. Hoo and I walked back to our blanket the women had packed the car. The four of us got in the car for the short ride up the street to Mr. Hoo's house. I told Mr. Hoo and his family that the enjoyable time I had that day. I let them know how honored I was to spend the day with them. We arrived back at Mr. Hoo's house, and I said good bye before heading back to the base. I spent the rest of the day writing letters in my bunk bed glowing about how wonderful life was for me.

The next month or so I spent learning the ropes that a supply Sergeant needed to know to do his jobs effectively. I spent most if not all of my time cleaning and inventorying the shelves of supply. Just as I was finishing the inventory, the fiscal year was coming to an end--budget time. One day the Gunny gave me some papers with numbers on them. "This is the budget. We have thirty days to spend this amount." the Gunny explained. I looked in disbelief. I had just documented a supply room with more stock than this unit could use in one hundred years of continuous war. I asked "Why?" The Gunny told me, "The unit is given a budget. If they don't spend it then they loose it." The budget for the next year is reduced by the amount not spent. I looked at the numbers on the paper and was amazed they wanted me to spend this amount of money. The Gunny told me to let him know when I was finished spending the budget money.

Kimko and I were spending all of our off time together each day. Sometimes we would just walk and talk. Other times we would go on trips. I saw most of southern Japan traveling with Kimko holding my waist tight riding on the bike. Kimko would explain everything to me about Japan and their culture. I could not remember on the short term but this did not seem to bother Kimko. I enjoyed just talking and being with her as she did me. We were in Hiroshima one day as she described the damage to the city during World War Two. Time was growing short for me as my tour in Japan was coming to an end. Our emotions were binding us closer and closer with each moment together. Kimko knew I had only a few months left in the Marine Corps. She could see my time with her in Japan was coming to an end shortly. On the Hiroshima trip I wanted to talk about some decisions I made. I told Kimko how I was going to reenlist in the Marine Corps so I could stay in Japan. The thought of leaving her was my reason to stay and spend my life with her. Kimko put two fingers to my lips and said, "I speak."

Kimko started telling me a story of the year before I met her. She had been in love with another Marine. Her father did not like this Marine, but she defied her father's wishes. This Marine was everything to her. Kimko described how she had long black hair down to her waist just one year ago. She went on telling me how this Marine loved to run his hands through her hair whenever he was near her. The feelings she felt for this man when he touched her in this way pleased her. She gave herself to him. I asked her what she meant, "gave her self." Kimko said, "I shamed myself." She gave her body to this Marine and he dumped her. Her mother cut her hair because when a woman in Japan is shamed, they can no longer have long hair. I asked Kimko if we were friends. She told me we were good friends. My mouth just started describing how I felt and my feelings for Kimko. I went on to tell her how much her friendship was a part of me. I told her my feelings were telling me more than I could understand with my mind. Kimko put her lips to mine and gave me a deep passionate kiss. I felt warm and glowing inside as our lips touched. The night was getting late so we headed back to the base after a short time.

The long ride back was different on this trip. Kimko's arms were around my waist but I could not feel the snug fit of her body as I had before. Her voice never sang a song in my ear. Our helmets never tapped as a drummer. I thought of these things on the ride, but assumed Kimko must have fallen asleep. I stopped the bike in front of her house. I noticed as Kimko got off the bike that she had tears running down her cheeks. The front of her shirt was wet enough to see through. I was confused and looked to see if a flying rock or stick might have hurt her. I gave her a hug and held her tight. She leaned her head back and put two fingers to my lips. I released my arms as Kimko took one step back from me. She told me, "We friends," and paused before saying, "You good friend and I want you very much. You respect me. You no try to go too far. I shamed family. I no be more than friend my whole life. Go please." The hour was late. I thought Kimko needed to think about what we talked about earlier today. I decided to head back and talk to her in three days when I was off from work again. I started back to the base on my bike.

The bike cruised down the road on its own path. I say this because I have no memory of the trip. I had so much happening my mind just went blank. I just cruised down the road two kilometers to the railroad tracks, then back to Kimko's street. I had no idea where I was. I was still on Kimko's street because I never turned to get one street over to the main gate. I was confused and lost. In Japan the railroad tracks are considered a stop sign. All vehicles including pedal bikes must come to a complete stop before crossing. The witness told of seeing me travel many times up and down the street. The last time down a car stopped in front of me at the tracks. The car brake lights woke me up from the daze that I was in. The tire of the bike bumped the rear of the car making a black mark on the car bumper. The old man got out of his car and was yelling in Japanese at me. I could tell he did not like Americans. I said, "Go menisci" which is Japanese "for sorry about that," then I left to go back to the base. The situation made me forget about Kimko ending our relationship, so I headed for the main gate.

I got to the main gate to find the Military Police and Japanese police waiting for me. Everything went crazy. The Japanese police pulled me off my bike and put me in the back seat of the police cruiser. Blue lights flashing, I was on my way to the Japanese police station. I tried to explain once we were inside the station, but no one spoke English.

The hours passed and finally a Marine Captain showed up. He spoke Japanese enough to sign some papers and get me back to the base.

I was placed on barracks arrest. This meant I could go to work at the unit and to the barracks. I was allowed to go to the mess hall and laundry building. I had a Military police escort whenever I went anywhere. I had no phone or any other privileges. I wanted to tell Kimko of my situation but I couldn't get in touch with her. I had friends bring messages to the bookstore, but she was not there any more. The routine of my restrictions became normal after the second week. I had forgotten the desire to do anything other than what I was allowed to do in compliance with the restrictions. I would just exercise, write letters, watch television, and work. The Marine Corps and Japanese police investigated that night for about thirty days. The day finally came a Captain told me I was going to Japanese court on three charges. The police report sheet said I was reckless driving, failure to stop at railroad crossing and alcohol. I would stand in front of a Premiere (Japanese Judge) tomorrow.

This was my last day of work in the supply room. I had been working on the budget list of supplies for thirty days now. I thought the Marine Corps needed a wake up call to the budget process. Anyway, I was going to jail, so why not make them think of me? I ordered two hundred and twenty seven thousand dollars of metal washers. I filtered the paperwork through the correct departments over the last week or so. I thought about how, once I am long gone; this unit will get thousands of excess washers that they will never use. I figured they would fit in the over stocked supply room with all the other useless things up there now.

The day of my court date came. I dressed in my Marine dress uniform. The Military Police were at my door to the second of the time designated. We drove for about an hour. The courthouse was one of those Japanese temple type buildings. It had the hand carved trim around the building inside and out. I thought of Kimko at that moment. I could hear her in my mind explaining the meanings of the Japanese culture to me as if she were there beside me. I had totally forgotten about her being in my life. Now I was remembering again. I had a desire to see her, but then my troubles flashed back into my mind. I was going to Japanese jail. I started thinking, trying to remember what happened that night. One memory would trigger another memory. I knew I was in trouble but I just accepted this as my path to travel. Was this real or a dream, I asked myself?

We entered the courtroom, which was packed with Japanese people all looking at me. I was directed to a table in the front where the Judge would sit. I turned to sit when I saw a row of high-ranking Marine Officers off to one side. The trial started as the people speaking Japanese started moving around the table. The Marine Captain who signed me out of the Japanese police station was sitting beside me. His job was to interpret everything said for me to understand. The trial lasted about an hour and there were no exciting parts. I think I was found guilty, but I don't know. I lost track of what was happening in my mind as I sat there in the room. I had no idea where I was, never mind what was happening in the courtroom.

The row of officers stood up and walked to the door of the room. That is when the Military Police escorted me to where the officers were standing. I was ordered by the Military Police to follow the officers to their cars. Once at the car I was ordered into the back seat with two high ranking officers sitting in the front seat. One officer was driving while the other sat quietly in the passenger's seat. I was driven directly to the runway on the Marine base. The car stopped at the steps leading up to the door of a C-117. The first words these two officers said were, "You saved our lives in Thailand. Have a good life Sergeant Macdonald." I got on the plane to find everything I owned was packed and on board waiting for me. The pilot handed me my orders with the comment, "Sergeant, you must really have connections to get a private flight at the last moment." I left Japan in a state of confusion.

Chapter Eighteen: Back to the World

I was so confused at this point in my life. My mind could not understand such changes that were happening around me. How did I get on a plane that was about to land on Guam Island? I had gone from being on my way to Japanese jail for three years to a plane ride back to the world, my world, the United States. My sense of reality was lost. The questions I kept asking related to what had just occurred a few hours earlier. I still had ninety days left to do in the Marine Corps. Where would I go? Why did Kimko dump me? I was having a hard time believing I belonged anywhere. My mind was flashing thoughts of past events that I did not understand. At that moment I was sitting in a military transport plane in which every seat was occupied. There were men from every branch of the United States Military Services present on this plane. My seat became an island where a Marine Sergeant sat in deep thought. I stayed awake for the entire flight but never heard a word spoken by anyone. I sat in silence with the belief this Marine needed to die.

The plane landed in Guam for a one-hour refueling stop on its way to Australia. I was to catch the another flight to Hawaii, which was scheduled to leave Guam in three days. Arrangements had been made so that I could be assigned a room for my stay on Guam. The flight crew quarters was located near the NCO club which was just fine by me. I had one hundred dollars in my pocket that was saved for my emergency needs. I had nothing left in life to live for. I would drink away the time. I noticed the NCO club had just opened when I was putting my bag in the room. The club was empty when I arrived. It appeared I was their first customer that day.

The club looked like any other military club, but I did not care. Everything was in its place and shined like it had been spit polished cleaned. All this military protocol did not matter to me. I just wanted a drink. I waited at the bar sitting on a tall stool playing with the peanut bowl. The bar tender failed to appear which made me impatient. The door to the storage room was open. I walked through this door yelling "Anyone here?" A voice sounded from behind the boxes of alcohol. "I'm over here." I looked on the floor and there was a man picking up broken glass that was spread all over the place. Getting involved was a natural event for me. I helped the man for about an hour cleaning up the mess. We took the unbroken bottles out of the boxes and put them in dry boxes. Wiping up the liquid was next. I got a mop to soak up the liquid material off the floor. I then washed the floor with soap and water before sitting back down on the barstool.

The bartender asked me what I was drinking. The memory of the turmoil in my life flashed back in my head. It was a mad rush of events filling my mind all at once. I went from content to someone trying to answer a million questions and stuck on the first question. Who was I? Was life real? The bartender started to talk to me as if we were friends. I did not want to talk to him or anyone else at first. I finished my first drink of whiskey in a few seconds after the bartender set it down. Not having time to move he asked if I wanted another drink. The bartender started talking to anyone who would listen. I was the only person in the room. I asked him why he was talking. He told me it helps when things go wrong for him. This started a conversation between us as the bartender handed me another drink. What do you think is best? How do you feel about it? The bartender was trying to draw my feeling out of me. The questions from the bartender kept coming. I felt like I'd heard this all before. The day turned to night and the bar started to fill up with other customers. I lost track of everything happening to me due to the amount of drinks. I don't remember where I was or what I did for the next three days.

I was sitting on a military transport half way to Hawaii when my mind woke up. I occupied the seat in the middle of the middle row on a plane. I had two Marine Corporals on each side of me. "Good afternoon," one of the corporals said to me. I looked around, wondering where I was. Then another Corporal stated, "You must have really tied one on." The others kept asking questions but I didn't even know who I was, never mind what was happening in my life.

The four corporals explained how their flight landed for a one-hour stop. They were sitting around the waiting area when a Gunny questioned them. One of the Corporals went on to explain that how the Gunny's questions was if we were on this flight to Hawaii. We said yes and he asked us for a favor. The surprise of a Gunny asking a favor shocked them in a way that made them say yes. The Gunny explained how a Marine did a favor for him at the NCO club, so he owed this Marine a favor. The corporals went on to explain when two privates came around the corner holding me up by the arms all their questions were answered. The Corporal's explained how they placed me in this seat with no sign of life until now.

Exhausted, my conscious state only lasted about thirty minutes and I slept the rest of the way to Hawaii, which did not seem to me to be a long flight.

I felt a relaxing feeling when the plane landed in Hawaii and the doors opened.

We were walking off the plane into a picture perfect story land. I was in paradise. I felt a joy to look around at all the different types of flowers. I had a peaceful joy come over me as I sat motionless in a chair looking at the trees sway behind a pool of water. The pool had water shooting straight up out of a fake tropical fish's mouth. The spout of water caused ripples that bumped the lily pads flowing in the pool. My eyes were open as crowds of people passed in front of me. The time couldn't have been but an hour when the four corporals came back with coffee and donuts for me. I had no sooner finished the snacks than we five Marines were back on the plane, leaving Hawaii behind us.

The plane ride to San Diego lasted seven hours. We had a smooth take off and landing, and that is the most I can say about that flight. At San Diego Marine Base we were taken by bus from the terminal to the staging area near the door to the temporary housing units. A boot Lieutenant put us in platoon formation and called us to attention. The thirty-three men in the platoon were made up of one sergeant, four corporals, and the rest were lower grades of Marines. The Lieutenant went through a checklist of instructions. All men with orders to be stationed at San Diego stand here he said. Those men to be stationed at San Diego left, leaving twenty-three men at the muster. The lieutenant then handed out sleeping section numbers for bunks in the building. The bunks were all in the same wing on the same floor. The Lieutenant then asked did any one have less than ninety days left on active duty. The order was then read anyone with less was eligible for earlier release from active duty. The four Corporals and I all stepped forward at the same time. The rest of the men were dismissed from the platoon. The next hour we stood listening to the Lieutenant speak on how great the Marine Corps was for our future. The five of us were all returning from long tours over seas. There was little chance we would reenlist in the Marine Corps. The Lieutenant finished his speech with the question will you sign here? "No Sir," came loud and clear from the five NCO's. The lieutenant tried to convince us by offering liberty for the weekend, or the other choice was fire watch in the barracks. Fire watch is a type of night patrol to control illegal act or disruptions during sleep time.

I spoke up as Senior NCO present. "No sir, Marine orders clearly state NCO's are exempt from fire watch except when lower ranking Marines are not available, sir." I had no idea if there was a Marine Corps order or not that said that. I said the sentence with force, in a clear voice. The lieutenant responded. "Sergeant, I am an officer. You take orders from me; do you understand?" I responded that, "I understood that the officer was wrong." I saluted the officer and asked to be dismissed. The five of us ignored the Lieutenant's orders and went out the main gate. The first thing we did was to rent a car.

We rented a four door Chevy Impala and drove in a direction away from the base. The first stop was the beach to look for those round-eyed California girls. A gift of life appeared in front of our eyes. We saw a large group of beautiful American girls in bathing suits. There was a bonfire glowing on the beach with a group of mostly girls gathered around it. The five of us dressed in our PX civilian shorts, sneakers, and tie-dye tee shirts walked up to the area and started talking. The crowd accepted us like they knew we belonged there. We ate hot dogs and chips, and drank their beer freely. No one seemed to care. The girls started talking more openly with us. The number of girls was three to every male on the beach. I mean these were dream round-eyed girls, dressed in bathing suits or mini skirts and tight tee shirts. These were the girls who could have been on the centerfolds that hung on our walls overseas. The picture type girls we dreamed about while waiting those long boring hours to complete a mission. While overseas we knew we were going to die in the process of doing our jobs, the dreams made accepting the fact easier. These girls at this time started hanging all over us trying for a good position to corral one of us. As we talked, the number of girls increased. America was better than my dreams could imagine! I broke away from the group to try to decide if what was happening was a dream or real life. I went to the car, which was about fifty feet away. I leaned against the front fender just looking around. The noise I heard was all voices that I could understand. These people were all speaking my language. The accents were different in each voice, but the tone of those American words bubbling out from those soft sweet voices made me feel good. I could hear some words plan as day when the tone of the words were constant. The voices as the person got excited would change frequency. I would not hear a high or low tone voice anymore. The other voices would fill in so it was a never-ending sound of an American crowd.

The hour was nearing 0400 as the number of people on the beach got less and less. My four friends were dancing and talking to four ladies around the fire. Off to one side near the radio were six boys drinking beer while they talked. The three girls with them were just standing silent with disgusted looks on their faces. I had a big smile on my face just scanning everywhere with my eyes. Was I really back in the world? I kept silently asking myself, could I really believe this is true?

I could see one of the three girls with the boys look my way. The thought of her looking at me never entered my mind. She started slowly walking toward me. My eyes were moving from side to side trying to see every girl in the area. She slowly broke away from the group and turned her back to where I was standing. I was trying to read a sign (written in English) just past where she was standing. I would catch little things she did at different locations that she would pause at. Her long slender legs sticking out from her ever so short red skirt. This kept my eyes going back for more peeks. She took a step moving further away from me. Her next step was like a dancer stretching her leg to one side for everyone to see. Slowly she turned flicking sand with her toes. My eyes were torn between her legs and my dreams. I would glance at her more frequently as the minutes pasted. She was completely turned looking at her own feet as she stretched each leg to close the distance between us. The fire had burned down to a glow of ashes as she reached its edge. Never looking in my direction her legs circled the fire. She knew my eyes were caught with interest. She glanced over at the six boys and walked in my direction at a noticeable intent.

The first word out of my mouth was "Hi." She was no more than six feet from me. She smiled and said, "I'm Barbara, but every one calls me Barbie." I told her how she had a pretty smile. I wasn't lying but any American girl would have looked good to me at that moment. Just then one of the boys looked over at Barbie and me. I heard him use unpleasant words calling for Barbie to get back where she belonged. Everyone turned and was now looking in my direction. Two of the boys started walking toward Barbie and my location with one of them still muttering some words.

My four friends still talking to the last remaining girl left at the fire went on alert. Everyone was turned in my direction watching the two boys walk toward me. I now could understand the words. He was yelling at Barbie. "You're my girl. You do what I say." I put my hand up, saying, "Calm down; we are just talking." The boy stopped yelling at Barbie at that point. He started telling me how he was going to kick the what ever out of me. I stopped leaning on the car and advised the boy, "Maybe you should rethink getting into a fight." The boy was now about six feet from where Barbie and I were standing. I made a fist in preparation for the events that were about to happen. I was about to push Barbie behind me when the boy doubled over in pain. I looked with a shocked expression on my face. Barbie was pulling her foot out of this boy's crotch. Barbie gracefully in a soft voice said, "I've had enough of you. Get away from me." The boy was down on his knees. He was buckled over in serious pain. I yelled to my four friends, "let's go." Barbie and the other girl asked what direction we were going? One of the other Marines told the girls to LA and back to kill the weekend. The two girls wanted to go with us. And so we were off to Los Angeles.

We drove up the free way for a couple of hours, but the distance traveled was not that far. The time must have been around 0900. We all felt it was time to stop for coffee and food. Barbie and Carol told us of a hotel they knew that was near by. They said we could eat, drink, and swim at this place. We took the next exit off the freeway. In a short time we were in the parking lot of a large resort hotel. Barbie and Carol seemed well aquatinted with the resort. We went through a back door into a pool house. Barbie got five men's swimsuits off a shelf. The swimsuits had the hotel name on them. Barbie told us they were complementary from the hotel for the guests to use. All of our clothes and other things were placed in a locked area for security. We were off to the pool for fun.

We walked past the main lobby when Barbie asked us to wait there for a minute. She and Carol then walked over to the reservation desk with a casual look. Carol started talking to the clerk while Barbie placed her elbows on the counter facing back into the room. A hotel guest came up from behind Carol. He said his name as he put his room key on the counter. Barbie and Carol came back to us a short time after the guest left the lobby and lead us through a door. Out to the pool we went. Barbie and I jumped in the pool first thing. Carol and the four friends got a table and called a waitress over. Barbie and I got tired of swimming after about an hour. We got out of the pool to join our friends. The table was filled with drinks and food when we got to it. Two of the men were sleeping still with drinks in their hands. One was in the pool swimming alone and the other had gone in the bushes with Carol. I was nervous about the bill from what I saw on the table. The time was about 1600 hours and the amount of things we had consumed was crazy. I asked Barbie to check on what we owed. I told her we had limited funds and that I was worried. Barbie said she would check. She got up from the table and hurried off to the lobby. Carol had been disappearing into the bushes with each one of my friends all day. I had Barbie to talk to all day, so I never thought to ask any questions.

It wasn't five minutes before Barbie was back with a nervous look on her face. She told us her cousin worked here and he would pick up the tab. She went on to explain how her cousin's boss just came back and will fire him if he finds non-guests around the pool. Carol and Barbie had us in the pool-house within seconds. The five of us went to change into our clothes but the girls stopped us. Carol said the hotel gives the suits away as the girls guided us out the back door. We were on the freeway again heading to LA

We made it to the city at about 2000 that night. Carol talked about this live music dance party she could get us in. We had been in the resort bathing suits all day, so we need to change. We stopped in a parking lot and put our clothes on. The girls put their mini shirts and Tee shirts over their suits. We walked across the parking lot to a large brick building. The line of mostly girls outside the door seemed endless. Carol walked up to the man standing in front of the door. The man talked into a phone then said something to Carol. Carol guided us down an alley to a door on the opposite side of the building.

The place inside was huge. The ceiling height must have been thirty feet. The place reminded me of an aircraft hanger with a twelve-foot high performance stage in the middle. Tables, chairs, and crowds of people filled the room. Waitress's running back and forth serving beer to whomever wanted it. The deal was your ticket cost two hundred to get in the door. This price gets you live music from nine, P.M. to five, A.M, plus all the beer you can drink. Carol's boyfriend was manager of the building, so he let us in for free.

Carol and Barbie used us for a free ride to get to this party. The joke was on them, I thought. We had heard Carol speak when she described how she got to LA to her boyfriend. I believe the words I heard were, "These dumb Marines were coming to LA so we hitched a ride for free." Carol and Barbie went to the bathroom so I told the others what was said. We laughed and glowed about the fact that the only money we had spent so far is car and gas. The girls came back in a while for more fun. We drank and danced the night away. The time was 0500 when we got back on the freeway. We drove for a couple hours to beat traffic before stopping at another resort Carol said that another cousin worked at.

The day went the same as Saturday had gone. We ate, drank, swam and slept the day away. Carol hurried us out of this resort earlier in the day than the day before, but we didn't mind. On the trip back Barbie and Carol were laughing and giggling. One of the other guys asked, "What's up?" Carol then explained to us how they used the name of a hotel guest and charged everything to that guest. They would keep an eye out for the guests to return, then leave the resort. We all laughed together during the ride as we ended up back at the beach where we started. There was a group of people around a fire getting ready for another night of partying.

This beach party was much the same as the first one. The difference this night was Barbie holding my hand all the time. About half way through the night she started talking about where I would be living. She wanted top know if I was going to be stationed in California. I had no idea what track my life would take. Then she wanted to know if she could write me. I had kissed her a few times over the weekend and it was nice. "What's up?" I asked. She told me I treated her with respect and she liked that. The men in California use women. I wasn't like that. I had gone the whole weekend without trying to get in her pants. She thought that meant I wasn't after just one thing. We talked about that subject and other things in life until 0430. The time for us Marines to leave had come. The five Marines hopped in the car and said good bye to everyone. We thought after we checked in to the base we would be back. The girls arranged with us to meet on the beach that night. Off to the base we went to check in.

The five of us cleaned and dressed for 0730 muster. The lieutenant wasn't too happy with the five of us. He started reciting the UCMJ (Uniform Code of Military Justice). He spoke in a clear, loud voice and every word that came out crushed my head with pain. The lieutenant added the charge of reporting for muster drunk. "Sir," I said, "These men (the four corporals) are my subordinates. I am responsible for their actions." The officer went on a marathon verbal degrading of my standing as a Marine Sergeant. I had served almost four years. I grew up in the Marine Corps (mentally) as far as I knew. I was getting out of the Marine Corps. The feeling that I had been through all this before came over me.

The base commander approached from a short distance away. The lieutenant called the men to attention. The Colonel and Lieutenant saluted each other. The formal military courtesy was completed before the two officers stepped away talking quietly to each other. I could see the Colonel slap an open record book between his hands. The Colonel was gesturing something to the Lieutenant. I could hear a loud word now and then about belittling a NCO in the presents of junior grade men. The conversation lasted a good thirty minutes before the two officers returned.

Still standing at attention the Lieutenant called, "Sergeant Macdonald, front and center." I approached in the Marine way of a step and turn march. I stood front and center between the two officers. The Colonel began by stating how my record book showed I had never been in trouble. I was promoted early or on time in rank. I was an excellent Marine according to my record book. I acknowledged the statements with a "Yes sir." The Colonel went on telling me about a good Marine's future with the Corps. He never asked me to reenlist. Before he handed me my discharge orders, he asked "Why did you defy an order on your last day, Sergeant?" I replied, "Sir my men and I were given the option to reenlist or stand fire watch. I am a Marine sir. The Marine Corps stands for glory not weakness sir." I was discharged from the Marine Corps with a handshake from the Colonel.

I stood at attention while the other twenty-three men received their orders. The five of us got back in our rented Chevy Impala and were off to the airport. I was lucky when I got to the airport the flight to Chicago had open seats and was leaving in five minutes. I boarded the plane after the getting a ticket and running down the loading ramp. I sat in an aisle seat with two other passengers between the window and me. I didn't have time to change out of my Marine dress uniform, which made me feel uncomfortable. I learned the couple next to me was returning from their honeymoon in Mexico. The girl was fascinated with my rank as a sergeant in the Marine Corps. I wasn't sure if I had caused the tension between the two of them or something else did.

The girl looked pretty with her long soft red hair. She had on a skintight net sweater and long skirt. I tried to talk to her husband, but he acted mad at everything I said to him. The stewardess started serving drinks now that we were in the air. The girl and I were having a great time drinking shots of whiskey and laughing. During the next hours I learned the couple had a fight on their last day in Mexico. This red headed bride was going to teach her husband a lesson by not paying any attention to him. While we waited for the stewardess to bring another drink, the girl looked at me in a strange way. She looked at her husband sitting beside us possibly sleeping and turned back to me. Then she wrapped her arms around my neck and started kissing me. Hey, I enjoyed it. We just continued making out for an extended amount of time. She had soft but moist lips.

At an unexpected moment the husband jumped up to a standing position looking down at us. The loud words out of his mouth brought the attention of the passengers from entire plane. This man was big. He must have been six inches taller than me and may be twenty-five pounds heavier. The man made a fist in one hand and reached for me with the other. I automatically sprang to my feet drawing my arm from behind his wife's head. My fist was placed firmly against his jaw, driving his head against the wall. The man was out like a light. The wife went crazy yelling at me, "How could you hurt my wonderful husband?"

The stewardess arrived to hear the wife talking about how she loves her husband. The wife kept implying I was to blame for their problems. The stewardess, having watched the situation from the beginning, asked if I would come with her. I stood in the galley for the rest of the flight. I drank and talked to the stewardess for the next hour until we landed at O'Hare airport in Chicago.

I changed planes there for a flight to New York from Chicago. I arrived in New York where I caught a flight to Boston, Massachusetts a short time latter. I had no idea where I was or how to get to New Hampshire once I was in Boston. I asked a ticket agent about New Hampshire and how to get there. The man sold me a ticket to Gilford Airport in New Hampshire, claiming the Lakes Region is the place to go. This plane was a little twin engine propeller plane that held two people. I sat next to the pilot in the cockpit. The wind blew the plane up and down, back and forth the entire flight. We did finally land in a small airport a scary two hours later. The terminal was a small metal building that acted as an information booth with no employees. I knew that Alton was my destination, but where was Alton? I asked around when this person who knew me said my name. I looked at him and we started talking. The person told me he would give me a ride to Alton because he lived there too.

This man, "Harold," described how we were friends before I went in the Marine Corps. He further described the car accident I was in with him while on leave. The car hit a rock and trees when he failed to make a turn with the road. I had no idea of what he was talking about, but a ride was a ride. He told me that we entered Alton. Then he asked me if I was going to my parent's house. I had corresponded with the Alton high school guidance counselor the whole time I was in the Marine Corps. I had taken High school courses to get my diploma from Alton high school while overseas. I then got college advice on which courses to take through the mail. I knew that college was something that would be good for me. I asked Harold if I could be taken to the school. We drove in to the Alton High School parking lot. Then Harold led the way to Mr. Smith, the counselor's office. I waited in the outer office and this kid kept talking to me. The kid interrupted me several times before I asked him, "What is it?" Harold said, "Peter this is your youngest brother, Michael." I had no idea. I had no memory of ever meeting him before. I had been home on leave once after the accident but I had no memory of people. I knew his name because of the letters I received. I was beginning a whole new challenge of life I could see that. I would have to change from the structured environment of rules and work to civilian life. I was no longer a Sergeant. I was a citizen with no memory.